The BC Wine Lover's Cookbook

Spirit Ridge, Osoyoos

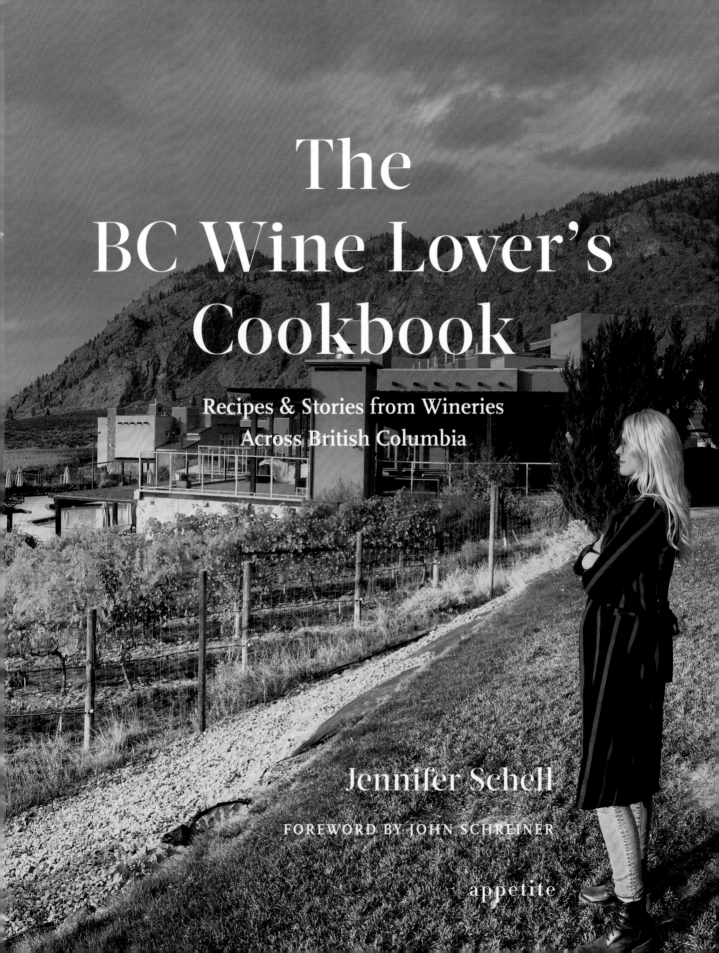

The
BC Wine Lover's
Cookbook

Recipes & Stories from Wineries
Across British Columbia

Jennifer Schell

FOREWORD BY JOHN SCHREINER

appetite

Appetite by Random House® and colophon
are registered trademarks of Penguin Random House LLC.

Library and Archives Canada Cataloguing in Publication data is available upon request.

ISBN: 978-0-525-61036-6
eBook ISBN: 978-0-525-61037-3

Photography by Jennifer Schell
Additional photography by: Tammy Renard: iii; Tracy Schell: 16; David McIlvride: 46, 48,
70, 72, 91, 92, 115, 116, 118, 120; courtesy of 8th Generation Vineyard: 78; Lionel Trudel:
102; courtesy of Meyer Family Vineyards: 114; Carmen Tomé: 140; courtesy of Le Vieux
Pin Winery: 145; courtesy of Checkmate Artisanal Winery: 156; Lee Murphy: 196.

Illustrations by Hillary Schell
Book design by Terri Nimmo
Printed and bound in China

Published in Canada by Appetite by Random House®,
a division of Penguin Random House Canada Limited.

www.penguinrandomhouse.ca

10 9 8 7 6 5 4 3 2 1

appetite
by RANDOM HOUSE | Penguin
Random House
Canada

To the mothers and grandmothers
who shaped our traditions, in the kitchen and around the dinner table,
and always added that secret ingredient:

Love.

Corcelettes Estate Winery (page 187)

Contents

Foreword
by John Schreiner

WINE IS GROWN TO ACCOMPANY FOOD, and books like this celebrate the connection between great wines and the foods they flatter. The fresh inspiration behind this particular book is that the recipes are generally not by chefs, but rather from the people behind some of British Columbia's best wineries. The profiles and recipes in these pages showcase the people who truly make the BC wine industry what it is today.

Numerous winery owners and employees have roots elsewhere in the world, and this has brought international expertise to our wine industry. (BC is, after all, one of the younger wine regions.) Bernd and Stefanie Schales, the owners of 8th Generation Vineyard, bring the knowledge of so many generations of German winegrowing. Their recipe, a *zwiebelkuchen* or onion quiche (page 81), is a traditional Schales family dish made to celebrate a new harvest.

The first recipe in the book is a shrimp ceviche from Federico Gonzales (page 15), a vineyard worker who comes to BC from Mexico for every harvest. This is a reminder of how vital Mexican workers are in BC vineyards and how international our wine and food culture has become. Tibor Erdelyi, the Serbian-born winemaker at Kalala Organic Estate Winery, contributes a recipe for hearty Hungarian goulash (page 65). Handed down in his family, it reflects his Hungarian ethnicity. It will also pair superbly with the full-flavoured reds that he and his peers make in the Okanagan.

This book is far more than a recipe catalogue. Jennifer, who also makes wine in the Okanagan with her two brothers, provides many illuminating details about the winegrowers behind the recipes. For example, the Coronation Grape Streusel Coffee Cake (page 45) developed by Susan Richardson of Sperling Vineyards enabled Jennifer to pull together important strands of wine industry history. Bert Sperling, Susan's father, supported the grape-breeding program that developed Sovereign Coronation, British Columbia's leading table grape. Sperling forebears, the Casorso family, planted Kelowna's first vineyards.

In *The BC Wine Lover's Cookbook*, Jennifer has woven history and biography together into a joyous celebration of our wines and our wineries in a book that reinforces the essential pairing of food and wine. Reading it made me eager to put on an apron, open a favourite bottle and start cooking.

Introduction

WELCOME TO BEAUTIFUL BC WINE COUNTRY! There are more than 370 wineries (and counting) across British Columbia, split between nine recognized wine regions: the famous Okanagan Valley, the Similkameen Valley, Vancouver Island, the Gulf Islands, the Fraser Valley, the Thompson Valley, the Shuswap and the newest regions, Lillooet and the Kootenays. These days, BC is known worldwide for its excellent wine, and as weather patterns change it is becoming possible to grow grapes ever farther north in the province. Which means more wine for all! Our wine world is full steam ahead.

We hear all the time that "great wine is made in the vineyard," and BC has an amazing range of vineyard soils. From desert to oceanfront, our diverse geography produces a huge spectrum of distinctive, terroir-driven wines. And the same goes when it comes to food! Farmers will tell you that vegetables have terroir, too. A carrot grown in one region does not taste the same as one grown somewhere else. It's all in the soil and the weather conditions unique to the area. Maybe that's why folks in the wine industry seem to have an instinct for which foods pair best with their wines. Or maybe it's because so many BC winemakers have a background in the culinary industry, including plenty of excellent chefs. With the province's incredible combination of farming, fishing, foraging and fine wineries, BC's food and wine are having one great love affair!

Wine drinkers in BC are absolutely spoiled for choice, and narrowing this book down to the wineries chosen was nearly impossible. I've tried to include a good range from across the province, with a mix of established and newer wineries. At each stop, you'll learn a bit about the history of the winery and winemakers, and what you'll find there when you go to visit. Then, I've shared one or two of their favourite recipes and the perfect wine to pair with them. The wineries in this book are organized geographically, so you could more or less drive from one end of the book to the next (map on pages 6–7), but you don't have to visit them that way! For wine tours built around your favourite varietal instead, have a look at my ideas for Wine Adventures on pages 262–274. Things change fast in the BC wine world, so give the wineries a call or check their websites before you plan a visit!

As part of the BC wine community myself, I know there is incredible diversity here, not just in our wines, but in the people behind those wines as well. In this cookbook, I wanted to showcase the beautiful cultures and nationalities that make up the community—Australian, Austrian, Canadian, Dutch, East Indian, French, German, Hungarian, Israeli, Italian, Kiwi, Mexican, South African, Swiss and more—all working together, and all sharing the dream to play a part in one of the world's most exciting new wine industries. And what better way to do that than through food? For recipes in the book, I asked the people behind each winery for a recipe that was meaningful to them. The recipes they provided are family favourites, from comfort food served after a long, hard day in the vineyard, to dishes prepared to celebrate the end of harvest. I love that some of these recipes came to me as a photocopy of a recipe card, some handwritten by a beloved grandmother. It has been a wonderful pleasure for me to connect with the families featured in these pages, and to collect together their favourite recipes in what feels like one gigantic international potluck party!

Through these recipes, we pay tribute to the spirit of the people they came from and the hours they spent in their kitchens preparing meals with love. For ideas on how to group the recipes together into menus, check out my suggested Seasonal Menus on pages 258–261.

I truly hope you enjoy these stories and recipes shared by some of the most wonderful, passionate people behind BC wine. Whether you plan to use this book as a keepsake from one of your favourite wineries, an inspiration to visit more or a way to bring a little bit of the BC wine world into your kitchen, this book is for you. My dream is that many of these dishes will become part of your own family's traditions and live on through the next generation of cooks.

A little note on the recipes: As you cook your way through, please assume that I recommend local and organic ingredients where possible, and (unless otherwise indicated):

Butter is salted	Milk is whole
Chicken, beef and pork are free-range organic	Olive oil is extra virgin
Cream is heavy	Pepper is fresh-cracked black
Flour is all-purpose	Salt is kosher
Herbs are fresh	Seafood is wild
Juice is fresh	Sugar is granulated

If you can, please plan a visit to the wineries featured in this book, and when you prepare their recipes, raise a glass of BC wine and thank them for sharing a little piece of their story. Cheers!

BC Wine Country Map

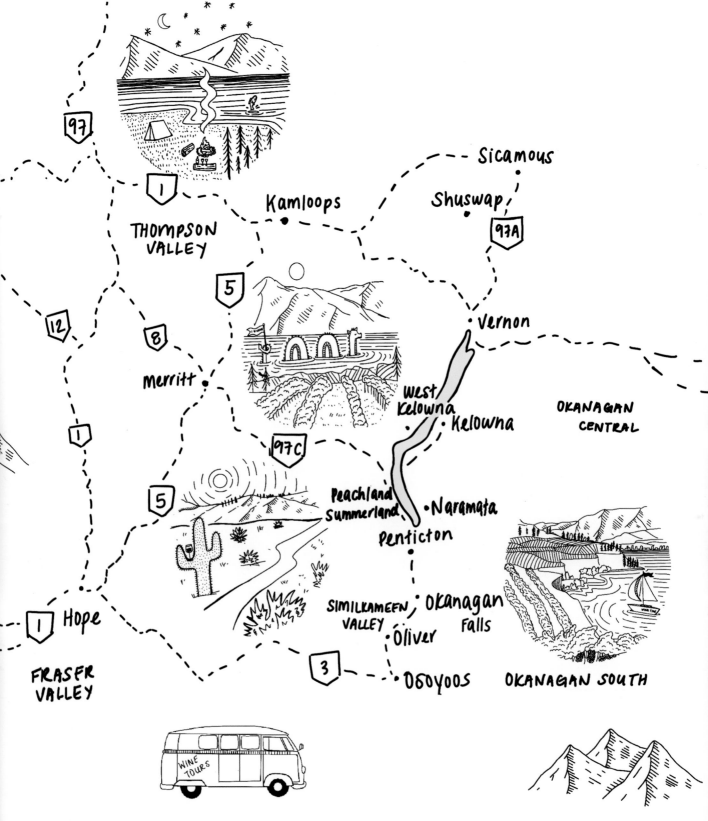

Quails' Gate Winery (page 51)

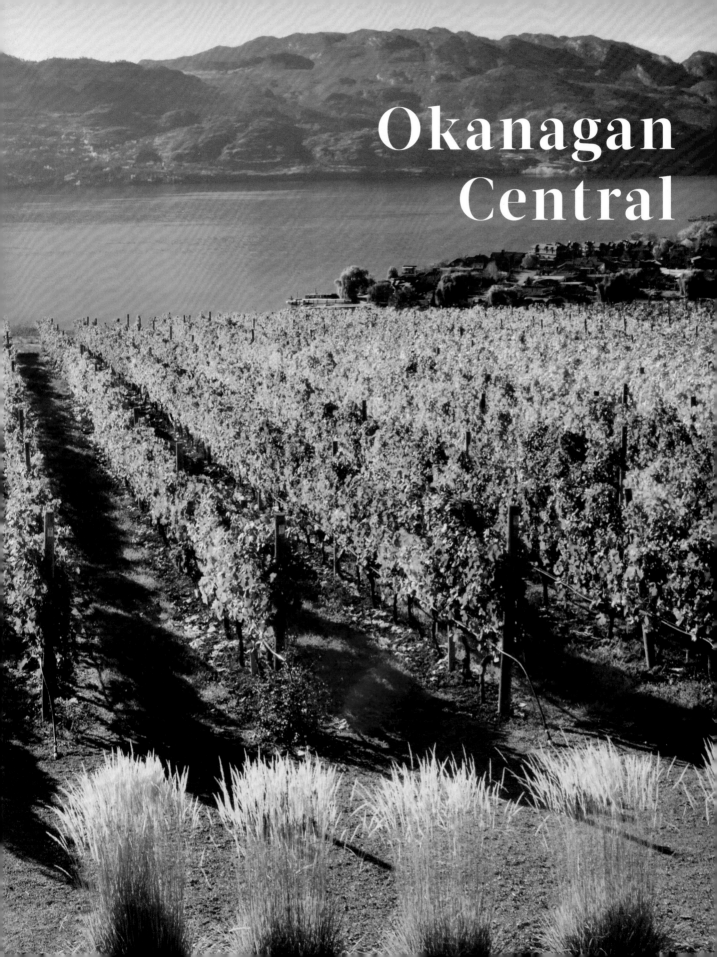

Okanagan Central

Lake Country

Kelowna

West Kelowna

Introduction

Extending from Lake Country to West Kelowna, the Okanagan Central area is filled with spectacular lakes. The glorious Okanagan Lake has a mystical quality and is said to be home to the Ogopogo, a legendary sea monster. The lake runs a remarkable 135 kilometres (84 miles) between Vernon and Penticton, graciously providing many sloping hillsides that have beckoned the wine savvy to plant vineyards. The largest city in the Okanagan, Kelowna, is a thriving urban centre that continues to expand outward, bringing the borders of Lake Country, West Kelowna and Peachland even closer.

Historically, Okanagan Central has been known for its deep agricultural roots and legendary Okanagan fruit. Rich orchards thrive between the vineyards and farms, providing a wealth of local produce. And much of that local produce is celebrated in the recipes of this book. There are food and wine events galore all year long, both within the Okanagan and at Big White, Kelowna's world class ski hill, an hour's drive away. The festive atmosphere of the entire area pairs very nicely with its status as a wine-country destination.

Outdoor enthusiasts will love the range of activities here, from water sports to hiking and mountain biking. Beach life and boating activities during the summer draw visitors from all over the world to revel in the heat of the Okanagan and enjoy the fun resort vibe of the area. At the spectacular Kalamalka Lake (just west of Okanagan Lake), mineral deposits below cause the water to reflect multiple shades of blue, earning it the nickname "the lake of a thousand colours." The fabulous Okanagan Rail Trail is a cycling trail that spans 49.5 km (31 miles) from Coldstream to downtown Kelowna, running alongside Kalamalka Lake. Stop along the way for a picnic and a dip in the colourful water!

Intrigue Wines

www.intriguewines.ca
2291 Goldie Road, Lake Country

Wine is intriguing! For wine aficionados it can be captivating, fascinating and even romantic. It can set a scene, alter a mood, enhance food and be a symbol of celebration. The passion for winemaking is perhaps even a little more intriguing once you understand the huge undertaking involved in this labour of love. When they were naming their winery, co-owner and winemaker Roger Wong's partners asked him what it was about wine that he loved so much. His response? "It's intriguing—it's constantly changing depending on farming, the weather and style." And the name of their winery was set!

After so many years of making wine, Roger knows what people like to drink. Intrigue Wines is known for their wide array of handcrafted wines at reasonable prices, and the fact that they offer wines for every palate—including bubbles! Roger and his partners wanted to inject some fun into, and take the pretension out of, wine drinking, so they opted to include some whimsical bottle designs along with the more serious ones and keep the prices accessible. Their cozy wine shop has loads of wine-themed gifts to choose from, making it a taste-and-browse kind of experience. And the lush picnic area outside is the perfect place to enjoy a delicious charcuterie board, also available in the wine shop, with your glass or bottle of wine.

Roger has been involved in the industry officially since 1995, and he was a garage wine-maker in his youth, making wine from kits. When he was growing up in Coquitlam, his family travelled frequently to Osoyoos, where he sourced some real grapes to play with . . . and he was hooked. To get his start, he volunteered at Tinhorn Creek as they were breaking ground with their new winery. "It was a fertile training ground where I learned everything from vineyard work to making wine and marketing," he remembers. Then, when he was at Gray Monk, he met Geri Davis, a solid presence in the BC wine industry with loads of experience.

As Jillian, Roger's wife tells it, "Roger and Geri were both working at Gray Monk—Roger as winemaker, and Geri as the controller. They had the crazy idea that after so many years in the wine industry, they should try to open up on their own. Our families found property in Lake Country and planted acreages in 2008." And they began to build the dream! A beautiful tasting room sits below Geri and her husband Ross's home and vineyard, and their garage is actually the crush pad for the winery!

Federico's Shrimp Ceviche

In the wine industry, crew is key when it comes to operating a successful winery. Many local wineries have had the good fortune of employing hardworking people who fly in from Mexico each year to get them through to harvest, and Intrigue Wines is no exception. Their crew returns every year with their captain, Federico Gonzales, and at the end of each harvest, they create a Mexican feast for the entire team to celebrate before they return home.

This ceviche is one of Federico's favourite recipes. It is a seafood dish typically made from fresh raw fish that is cured (cooked) in citrus juices. The goal is to have all the ingredients finely chopped so the pieces are uniform in size and it's easy to scoop onto tortilla chips.

Serves 8–10 as an appetizer

1 lb medium or large shrimp, cleaned, peeled, deveined and finely diced

1 cup + 2 Tbsp lime juice

1½ avocados, finely diced

3 firm Roma tomatoes, deseeded and finely diced (see note)

1 large jalapeño pepper, deseeded and finely diced (see note)

2–3 Tbsp cilantro, minced

½–¾ cup extra-spicy Clamato juice

Salt

Valentina Salsa Picante or other Mexican hot sauce (optional)

Tortilla chips, to serve

Notes: *For more spice, include the seeds and ribs of the jalapeños. Aim to use tomatoes that are just ripe—if they are overripe, the consistency of the ceviche can become too wet.*

Place the shrimp pieces in a large bowl. Add 1 cup of the lime juice to completely cover them. Set the bowl in the fridge and gently stir every 10–15 minutes, until the shrimp change colour from clear/grey to white with a pink hue, then finally to a light coral or orange, 30 minutes to 1 hour. Cut into a piece of shrimp to make sure it is opaque throughout and there are no translucent pieces.

Drain the shrimp and gently fold in the avocados.

In a large bowl, combine the tomatoes, jalapeños and cilantro, then add the shrimp and avocado. Add ½ cup of the Clamato juice and the remaining lime juice, and mix together. Add more Clamato juice to taste. Season with salt to taste.

Transfer to a serving bowl and top with salsa picante if desired. Surround with tortilla chips. ¡Buen provecho!

Pair with: Intrigue Riesling. This wine offers up aromas of peach, apricot and fresh apples. The crisp acidity delivers mouth-watering flavours of green apples, tangy lemon and honey. Cooler temperatures at night help to maintain the fresh acidity that great Rieslings are known for.

Schell Wines

www.garagistenorth.com
www.jenniferschell.com

The term "garagiste" was originally used to describe a group of renegade winemakers in Bordeaux, France, who became an international sensation when they broke the country's strict regulations on wine blending and winemaking to create something new. Today in BC, it is a way to describe passionate small-batch winemakers who produce under 2,000 cases of wine each and use only 100% BC grapes. After co-producing Garagiste North: The Small Producers Wine Festival for many years with my friend Terry Meyer Stone, I caught the fever and wanted in!

Like many who want to join the wine industry, I didn't have a winery, a vineyard or land to plant one, so I approached my two brothers, Jonathan and Jamie (yes, my mom liked the letter "J"), and asked if they wanted to become garagistes and do a custom crush. (A custom crush is when a licensed winery allows other wine brands to produce wine at their facility, usually using their own winemaker.) After all, we are farm kids—raised in a quasi-European household that made everything from scratch, including yearly wine-making with our opa. I hoped they would be interested, but I knew they were both very busy with their own families and the dental tech business that they operate together. To my surprise, they both enthusiastically said yes!

Number one on our to-do list was to find a winemaker, and we hit the jackpot with Rob Westbury of Nagging Doubt Winery, a garagiste who makes great wine and lives next door to Jamie. Number two: buy grapes. I am grateful for all of the relationships I have formed with wineries and grapegrowers over the last decade in the industry. After a couple of calls, voila! Supreme grapes to make a Chardonnay (my drink of choice) and a red blend (my brothers love the reds). My niece Hillary Schell is an amazing illustrator (her work is in this book!), and she designed our beautiful logo, which represents the family tree and our orchard history. And Schell Wines was born!

In 2017 we bottled our first wine, the 2016 Chardonnay. Sourced from an East Kelowna vineyard just over a mile from our home farm, where our parents still reside, the grapes are as close as we could get to making wine from our family terroir. 2018 brought our red blend, Ruby, named for our beloved Aunt Ruby, and our second vintage of Chardonnay, Wren. Future plans are for a red blend named for our great-grandfather Xeferius Schell.

As much as I thought I knew about the wine industry, this project has been an eye opener—especially financially, as you just cannot imagine all of the costs involved in creating wine: grapes, barrels, production, storage, labels, bottling, delivery, accounting . . . Please don't ask local wineries why we don't have $5 bottles of wine available in Canada! With the cost of land, production, labour, etc., it is simply not possible.

On the flip side, oh, what wonderful fun! To create your very own bottle of wine, with your family name on it, is just priceless. We are thrilled to be a small part of the burgeoning, exciting garagiste community. Cheers to the past and to the future!

Schell Family Crab Boil

The Schell family loves some crab. Since we were children, when our parents would take us out to the Keg and let us split a seafood platter, we have loved it all. The hot butter, the eating with your hands, the claw crackers. Those special nights ended when we all got big enough to demand our own seafood platter.

Many years ago, one of my best friends, Brent Beasley, cooked a crab boil for my birthday. We purchased a huge restaurant-size spaghetti pot with a built-in strainer from Italy and a gas burner to set up outside. The yard was filled with long tables with seating for 40, and Brent fed them all, and then some, with this now-famous family-favourite crab boil feast. That big old pot has gone on the road with me many times to create crab boils on Bowen Island, in Tofino and in various other locations. I have my kit of crab boil essentials in a box ready to go at any time!

If you are catching the crabs yourself, PLEASE ensure that you kill them humanely and follow BC crab harvesting laws. Alternatively, order them to be processed and picked up at the closest possible time to your meal.

Serves 12 (but can be adjusted to serve as many as you like—assume each person will have ½–1 crab, ½–1 link of sausage, 3 new potatoes, 1 cob of corn, ½ onion and 2 shrimp)

2 packages Louisiana Seafood Boil spice blend, or your favourite spice blend (check package for yield per boil)

8 lemons, halved, + more cut in wedges to serve

6 yellow onions, halved

36 new potatoes

6–12 mild Italian sausages, partially cooked

12 Dungeness crabs, humanely killed and ready to cook

12 cobs corn, shucked

24 large shrimp, shell on (optional)

12 ramekins filled with melted garlic butter, to serve

Sliced baguettes, to serve

Prepare your serving table by covering it with a thick layer of newspaper or water-resistant tablecloth.

Fill a 44-quart pot (enormous, I know!) just over halfway with water, keeping in mind that the ingredients will raise the water level significantly. Bring to a boil. Add the spice blend, lemons and onions, and let simmer for 10 minutes. Drop in the potatoes and cook until just fork-tender, about 7 minutes.

Add the sausages and bring back to a boil, then add the crabs, corn and shrimp (if using). Boil for 9 minutes, then remove the pot from the heat.

Strain your feast, then dump it directly onto the table! No forks or knives are necessary—roll up your sleeves and eat with your hands. Serve with melted garlic butter and plenty of sliced baguettes.

Notes: You will need crab crackers and picks to serve. You may also want to provide rolled-up damp, lemon-scented facecloths as an alternative to napkins.

Pair with: Schell Wren Chardonnay. This wine has pear, apple, peach and vanilla on the nose and palate, balanced acidity and an extremely long finish. Our winemaker uses minimal intervention and no additives—we let our grapes sing their own song. #Chardonnayism

CedarCreek Estate Winery

www.cedarcreek.bc.ca
5445 Lakeshore Road, Kelowna

Perched on the hillside of scenic Lakeshore Road, CedarCreek is one of Kelowna's oldest wineries and one of the original eight pioneering wineries in BC. It offers ideal growing conditions as well as a killer view of Okanagan Lake. The winery features stunning fieldstone walls and contemporary farmhouse buildings in a village setting that looks as though it has been part of the tree-lined 50-acre vineyard property forever.

In 2014 the von Mandl family purchased CedarCreek Estate Winery from the Fitzpatrick family and embarked on exciting changes and renovations for this special property. The brand is more glorious than ever, maintaining its original philosophies and adding an exciting new focus on organic farm practices. Winemaker Taylor Whelan and viticulturist Kurt Simcic are both passionate about organics, and their credo reflects stewardship of the land and sustainability in all ways possible.

Kurt was brought to the Okanagan from New Zealand for his expertise in helping vineyards make the transition to organic. He lets the land guide him on the best ways to nurture the vines and help them thrive. As au courant as his philosophies may sound, he is actually incorporating old-world organic farming techniques and fine-tuning his methods by focusing on individual blocks of unique terroir.

Taylor grew up in Campbell River on Vancouver Island. "My winemaking inspiration evolved over time, beginning when I was studying in Victoria," he says. "My interest in wine developed to further enhance the cooking and eating experiences I was playing around with at home. I love the process, starting with identifying unique or interesting sites in the vineyard, working with the viticulturists to farm those sites in a way that best expresses that uniqueness, and then making the wines with the same view. To me, being able to show site in the finished product is the most compelling part of winemaking."

The new restaurant on-site, Home Block, is named for the vineyard it rests upon. The building is crafted from the same fieldstone as the winery, and the interiors feature reclaimed 100-year-old barn wood. Chef Neil Taylor's modern Mediterranean menu explores Spanish and Italian flavours through the lens of the Okanagan. "We have the ideal climate to produce the ingredients that I love and feature on the menu," he says. As for the stunning lake-facing terrace, surrounded by vineyard and cedar trees . . . you may never want to leave.

Yida's Portuguese Chicken

CedarCreek's winemaker Taylor Whelan grew up on Vancouver Island. Each year, his family purchased a pig to be raised by his best friend's parents, Jim and Yida Scott. "Yida's family is Portuguese," explains Taylor, "and they made their own chorizo sausage from the pigs with heaps of smoked paprika, red wine and cumin mixed with the pork, smoked and cured. Over the years, my family adopted the recipe for this comfort-food dish. If I get an evening off during harvest, I can whip up a big batch without too much fuss, and it is even better the next day."

Serves 6

6–8 cloves garlic, minced

¼ cup olive oil

3 heaping Tbsp smoked Spanish paprika (see note)

1 Tbsp salt

1½ tsp pepper

1 (3–4 lb) roasting chicken, sectioned (see note)

1 cup dry white wine (preferably CedarCreek Sauvignon Blanc)

6 Sieglinde potatoes, halved

6 cured or semi-cured Spanish chorizo sausages, sliced into 1- to 2-inch pieces (see note)

Chopped flat-leaf parsley, to garnish

Notes: *To section the chicken, cut apart the legs, back pieces and breasts for a total of six pieces. If it's a large chicken, you may also want to separate the drumsticks from the thighs and halve the breasts. If you're not comfortable sectioning a chicken yourself, ask a butcher to do it for you.*

Make sure you purchase Spanish or Portuguese chorizo, not Mexican (which contains cumin), and use smoked paprika, not regular.

Preheat the oven to 375°F.

In a bowl, combine the garlic, olive oil, smoked paprika, salt and pepper. Roll up your sleeves and massage the mixture all over the chicken pieces—the longer the massage, the better the flavour! Pour the wine into the bottom of a large roasting pan, and top with the chicken pieces, arranging so they are all in one layer. Arrange the potatoes around them.

Roast, uncovered, until the chicken is just starting to brown, about 30 minutes. Remove the pan from the oven and add the chorizo pieces, distributing them around the chicken and potatoes. Turn the chicken pieces to allow for more even browning. Return the pan to the oven and cook until the juices in the chicken thighs run clear and the pieces are fully browned, about another 30 minutes.

To serve, divide the chicken, chorizo and potatoes between plates and top with the flavourful jus and a sprinkling of parsley. Serve with a crusty loaf of bread and a bright salad topped with almonds and blue or Manchego cheese and drizzled with sherry vinegar. Cheers!

Pair with: CedarCreek Sauvignon Blanc. This crisp wine cuts through the fat in the chicken and sausage, and the paprika makes the acidity race. You are left with a lovely clean finish.

Martin's Lane Winery

www.martinslanewinery.com
5437 Lakeshore Road, Kelowna

Martin's Lane Winery is one of the four distinctive wineries that make up the Anthony von Mandl empire. An astonishing work of art, this six-level gravity-fed winery was designed by Tom Kundig, the superstar architect who also designed von Mandl's Mission Hill Family Estate Winery and the pop-up building for CheckMate Artisanal Winery. This structure, though, is really out of this world. The attention to detail is amazing: the staircase in the entrance is crafted to the specifics of the Fibonacci spiral, and a six-foot-high bronze Douglas Coupland sculpture of Vincent van Gogh is dramatically positioned on its side, sans ear, beside the Pinot Noir vineyard, where it looks like he is listening to the ground to hear the grapes growing (see page 29). Coupland's *Project Redhead* was inspired by the fact that Pinot Noir and redheaded humans are both genetic mutations.

Details and a focus on excellence are themes that run throughout the Martin's Lane brand. Case in point: they concentrate on two top-tier varietals only, a Riesling and a Pinot Noir. The winery was named for Anthony's father, Dr. Martin von Mandl, and it is perched slightly above CedarCreek Estate Winery, another member of the empire. The site was chosen because of the brilliant terroir on this hillside of the Upper Mission area of Kelowna—and perhaps the breathtaking lake views were an inspiration too. Tastings and tours are by appointment only, but well worth the wait.

Shane Munn is a New Zealander who came to BC wine country with his family to become the general manager and winemaker of Martin's Lane. Shane's great passion for winemaking, Pinot Noir and organic and biodynamic viticulture made him the perfect fit for this exciting and sophisticated label. He has crafted wines at impressive wineries in New Zealand and eastern Canada and spent time in Barolo, Italy.

"Elegance and character are primarily what I look for in any wine," he says. And winemaking? "Detailed and uncompromising but mostly gentle and guiding."

Kathleen's Bibimbap

Kathleen Munn, wife of Martin's Lane's GM and winemaker Shane Munn, learned to make this popular dish while she was living in Korea. *Bibimbap*—which basically means "mixed rice"—is delicious (and extremely fun to say). It's the perfect combination of colour, texture and flavour and has become a favourite in the Munn household. "The gochujang sauce can be added as per your personal taste," says Kathleen. "It's a little spicy, but delicious!"

Serves 4

Gochujang Sauce:

4 Tbsp gochujang (hot pepper paste)

1 Tbsp honey

1 tsp sesame oil

1 tsp soy sauce

2 cloves garlic, minced

Sprinkle of sesame seeds

Beef:

2 cloves garlic, minced

1 Tbsp minced ginger

1 Tbsp honey

1 Tbsp soy sauce

1 Tbsp sesame oil

1 lb lean steak, like boneless rib eye, thinly sliced (you can ask a butcher to do this for you)

Bibimbap:

2 cups sushi rice

3 cups bean sprouts

1 cup julienned carrots

2 small zucchini, sliced

Pinch of salt

2 Tbsp olive oil

2 cups sliced mushrooms

1 clove garlic, minced

1 Tbsp sesame oil

1 tsp soy sauce

1 cup julienned bell peppers

2 tsp butter

4 eggs

For the Gochujang Sauce:

In a bowl, whisk together all the ingredients and set aside.

For the Beef:

In a bowl, mix together the garlic, ginger, honey, soy sauce and sesame oil. Stir in the beef and refrigerate for about 30 minutes until ready to cook.

For the Bibimbap:

Cook the rice according to the package instructions. Fluff with a fork, cover and set aside for serving.

Set out a platter for the vegetables, and place the sprouts on it. In separate bowls, mix the carrots and zucchini with a pinch of salt each and set aside for 15 minutes to draw out excess water.

In a wok or large pan over medium-high heat, heat 1 Tbsp of the olive oil and add the mushrooms. Sauté for 3–4 minutes. Add the minced garlic, stir-fry for another minute, then add the sesame oil. Cook for another minute, drizzle with soy sauce and toss. Remove the mushrooms and garlic to the vegetable platter.

Add the remaining olive oil to the wok and stir-fry the bell peppers for 2–3 minutes, keeping them crunchy. Remove them to the vegetable platter.

Use a paper towel to squeeze the carrots and zucchini dry. Add the carrots to the wok and stir-fry for 1 minute, then remove them to the vegetable platter. Grill the zucchini separately until charred, either on the barbecue or in a cast-iron grill pan. Remove to the vegetable platter.

Remove the beef from the fridge and stir-fry over high heat for 3–4 minutes. Remove from the wok and set aside.

continued

To Serve:

Sesame oil

2 green onions, sliced

Sesame seeds

Kimchi (Korean fermented cabbage)

Heat 1 tsp of the butter in the still hot pan, then fry two of the eggs (sunny side up!) and remove to a plate to reserve for serving. Repeat with the remaining butter and eggs.

To Serve:

Time to build the bowls! In each of four bowls, place a few drops of sesame oil. Divide the rice among the bowls, then arrange the sprouts and vegetables on top. Arrange the beef on top of the vegetables, then place an egg on top of the beef.

Sprinkle with green onions and sesame seeds, and serve with gochujang sauce and kimchi on the side.

Pair with: Martin's Lane Fritzi's Vineyard Riesling. Fritzi's Vineyard was named in honour of Anthony von Mandl's mother, Fritzi, when she celebrated her 100th birthday. This Riesling is entering a lovely period of early maturity, with a subdued nose showing a stony minerality, and a powerful, pure and dry palate.

Douglas Coupland's sculpture of Vincent van Gogh

Summerhill Pyramid Winery

www.summerhill.bc.ca
4870 Chute Lake Road, Kelowna

Visionaries, ambassadors, pioneers, musicians and leaders in the BC organic movement, Stephen Cipes and his family (wife Ria, sons Matthew, Gabe, Ari and Ezra, and daughter "EE" [Esther Ehisa Oshita Cipes]) fully support and live the organic and biodynamic lifestyle. "No herbicides or pesticides keeps the lake clean, and our grapes don't taste like chemicals," says Stephen. "Our wines are allowing nature to speak for herself."

Originally a New Yorker with a successful real estate development company, Stephen and his family embarked on their grand winery adventure in 1986, when they moved to the Okanagan and began to build Summerhill. The winery is home to an organic bistro, vegetable gardens, beehives, a Kekuli (a replica of the sacred winter home for the local Indigenous Peoples) and the magical pyramid. Built to reflect the Cipes family's deep spirituality and to act as a wine cellar, the pyramid shows the mystical effect that this legendary structural shape has on liquids. Every solstice and equinox, and on every full and new moon, there are community gatherings in the pyramid and Kekuli to meditate and celebrate our connection to the earth and universe. And then there is the bubble. Master winemaker Eric von Krosigk boasts multiple international award–winning sparkling wines.

Summerhill was the first winery in BC to achieve both Demeter Biodynamic certification and organic certification. "We add no yeast or nutrient and no fermentation or processing aids of any kind," Ezra explains. "We create the right environment for the juice to turn naturally to wine, and we monitor the process. At the end we clarify the white wine with bentonite and add a little sulphur as a preservative. That's it; that's all."

Raised surrounded by instruments and their dad Stephen's love of playing music, all of the Cipes children are talented musicians. Their family band, The Oot n' Oots, which performs kid rock, is made up of the four Cipes brothers and Ruth, Ezra and his wife Rio Branner's daughter, who has a powerful voice as soulful as a blues singer four times her age. Watch this girl's star rise!

Pair with: Cipes Brut NV. Made in the traditional method from organic Riesling, Chardonnay and Pinot Blanc, this brut has aromas of apple, lime, pear, almonds and grapefruit. On the palate, Cipes Brut exhibits crisp acidity, a soft, creamy mousse and a long finish, and has won gold medals every year since it was first released in 1992.

Summerhill Okonomiyaki with Smoked Salmon

Okonomiyaki is a type of Japanese savoury pancake that can be made with a variety of ingredients. In Japan, it is made in every household, and it is totally addictive. Ria Cipes is from Japan and loves to make okonomiyaki for her family. She creates a special heart-healthy version for Stephen (note below). Summerhill executive winery chef Jeremy Luypen helped create this delicious base recipe.

This recipe makes four medium-size portions or two large. If you are a beginner, divide the batter into four, and don't worry if your first one isn't perfect! You will get the hang of it.

Serves 2–4

1 cup flour
2¼ tsp sugar
¼ tsp salt
¼ tsp baking powder
¾ cup vegetable stock
1½ lb red or green cabbage, chopped into small pieces
4 eggs
¼ cup pickled pink ginger, chopped
2–4 Tbsp canola oil
½ cup mayonnaise
Sliced chives, to garnish
½ lb thinly sliced smoked salmon

Okonomiyaki Sauce
2 Tbsp ketchup
2 Tbsp Worcestershire sauce
1 Tbsp fish or oyster sauce

Note: To make Ria's heart-healthy version of this recipe, use tofu instead of eggs, and cook the batter in a nonstick pan with no oil.

In a large bowl, mix the flour, ¼ tsp of the sugar, salt, baking powder and stock until well combined. Cover with plastic wrap and refrigerate for 1 hour.

Make the okonomiyaki sauce. In a small bowl, whisk together the ketchup, Worcestershire, fish sauce and remaining sugar until the sugar has dissolved. Set aside.

Set the chopped cabbage on paper towel to remove the moisture.

Remove the batter from the fridge. In another bowl, whisk together the eggs and pickled ginger until well combined, then stir into the batter. Gently stir in the cabbage.

Heat 1 Tbsp of the canola oil in a medium-size frying pan over medium heat. Once hot, add a quarter of the batter mixture (or half if you are making two large servings) and spread into a circle on the pan. You can make it as thin or as thick as you like, but you should cook only one pancake at a time. Cover and cook until the bottom has browned, about 5 minutes. Flip over, cover and cook about 5 more minutes. Transfer to a plate, then repeat until all the batter is cooked, adding another 1 Tbsp oil to the pan before starting each pancake.

To serve, okonomiyaki is traditionally topped with okonomiyaki sauce and mayonnaise applied in a criss-cross design (squeeze bottles make this easy). Sprinkle with chives and arrange the smoked salmon on the plate.

SpearHead Winery

www.spearheadwinery.com
3950 Spiers Road, Kelowna

As you drive uphill into South East Kelowna's distinctive orchard district, a brilliant Provence-yellow winery will catch your eye. SpearHead Winery hit the BC wine map hard with their award-winning, estate-grown Pinot Noir and other finely crafted wines. Success with the so-called heartbreak grape (Pinot Noir) in this area has been phenomenal, and the special terroir at SpearHead is growing amazing fruit.

Winery owner Marina Knutson explains, "The South East Kelowna area is unique. The wineries are still within the city of Kelowna, but also in the Agricultural Land Reserve. That means that our tasting rooms are very close to the city and its amenities, but there are no big developments in the area. It's quiet, with few cars but lots of horses, tractors, orchards and vineyards. Guests are always a little surprised but very pleased to discover what a hidden gem South East Kelowna really is."

The estate's landscaping design includes a winery building ensconced in vines—a lovely setting with a view of the city in the distance. The Knutsons have hosted many events here, including some wonderful al fresco performances by Shakespeare Kelowna. There is a welcoming patio area with tables and colourful sun umbrellas to linger under. SpearHead is also part of the BC Pinot Noir Celebration, which has become a huge draw for Pinot Noir lovers and international wine media.

Marina and her husband Bill sort of fell into this life, she says. "We were approached by a friend who had found the property and had the idea of starting a winery. We had no idea what that involved, but we thought we would do it anyway. And here we are, 10 years later!"

They have recently expanded to a new facility that allowed them to double their production. They continue to focus on small-batch Pinot Noir, Chardonnay and aromatic whites—the perfect fit for superstar winemaker Grant Stanley (pictured here with his wife, Annabel). After a long, award-laden history of winemaking, Grant has found a new home at SpearHead. In his other role as general manager, he has brought great wisdom and vision to the brand and designed the new production facility. You will find him in there, classical music pumping, ablaze in his element.

Annabel's Greek Orange & Almond Cake

SpearHead winemaker Grant Stanley's wife Annabel is a trained horticulturist and an artist who creates stunning woven baskets (featured in the dish photo) and sculptures from harvested grapevines! This cake recipe is much requested at her family celebrations and is a new crush party tradition at SpearHead Winery. The recipe also has a romantic story attached: Annabel originally acquired it from a bakery in London she worked at as a young woman while trying to save money to travel to Australia, where she eventually met Grant. Enjoy!

Serves 8

Cake:
⅔ cup butter
½ cup berry sugar
Zest of 1 orange
2 eggs, beaten
1 cup semolina
¾ cup ground almonds
2 tsp baking powder
3 Tbsp orange juice

Syrup:
1 cup sugar
1-inch stick cinnamon
1½ Tbsp lemon juice
1½ Tbsp orange juice

To Serve:
¼ cup sliced or slivered almonds, blanched and toasted
1 cup clotted cream or crème fraîche
Edible petals (optional)

Notes: If you like, double the syrup for an even moister cake.

For the Cake:
Preheat the oven to 400°F. Grease an 8-inch springform pan and line the base with parchment paper.

In the bowl of a stand mixer fitted with the paddle attachment, cream the butter, sugar and orange zest until light and fluffy. Gradually beat in the eggs, beating well between each addition.

Fold in the semolina, ground almonds, baking powder and orange juice, then transfer the batter to the prepared cake pan.

Bake until the cake is golden brown and has shrunk from the pan sides, about 30 minutes. Allow to cool in the pan, then turn out onto a plate.

For the Syrup:
Meanwhile, in a small saucepan over medium heat, combine the sugar with 4 Tbsp of water and the cinnamon stick. Gently bring to a boil, and simmer for 5 minutes.

Remove from heat and discard the cinnamon stick, then stir in the lemon and orange juices. Let cool for 15 minutes, then pour the syrup over the cake. Cover and let sit for a few hours to give the syrup time to be absorbed.

To Serve:
Sprinkle with almonds and serve with a dollop of clotted cream or crème fraîche. If you like, decorate with edible petals.

Pair with: SpearHead White Pinot Noir. This rare wine is the result of making a white wine from red Pinot Noir grapes. It is an excellent food wine, with rounded edges that complement richer cuisine.

The View Winery & Vineyard

www.theviewwinery.com
#1–2287 Ward Road, Kelowna

The View Winery & Vineyard and its president, Jennifer Turton-Molgat, are a beautiful combination of farming and glamour. Jennifer has deep historical roots in the Okanagan's agriculture industry, and her fun and flirty winery branding has lifted them into the future and brought new sparkle to her story. She's not just the beautiful face behind the brand; she runs her company with moxie and the class of an impressive leader—one who also has a great sense of whimsy and humour. Case in point: the sexy red high-heeled shoe featured in the logo has a saucy story behind it—one that involved wine and dancing with her husband Kent Molgat.

Kelownians are very familiar with the Turton name, and before that, the Ward name. Jennifer's great-grandfather George Ward moved his family to the area from Birmingham, England, in the early 1900s, and in about 1920 he built one of the Okanagan's first fruit packinghouses on the South

East Kelowna property that he had purchased as an apple orchard. Jennifer's nana, who was born in the Glenmore area of Kelowna in 1911, grew up on the property, and later Jennifer's father Chris took over the family orchard business.

"In the 1990s my father Chris was approached by a local winery and asked if he'd like to grow grapes for them," Jennifer explains. "Around the same time, he had begun to explore opportunities in the blossoming apple cider industry. This was the beginning of the property's transformation from fresh market fruit trees to grapevines and cider apple trees."

In 2006 Jennifer and her dad opened The View Winery & Vineyard. The name makes perfect sense when you stand atop the vineyards and take in the absolute visual splendour of the lake and valley vista below. Taking advantage of the unique terroir of the property, they planted cool-climate, aromatic whites; Pinotage—a first for the industry—and cider apples. The View's rosé and sparkling wines have become consumer favourites, as has their progressive move into sparkling wine in a can. Aptly named Bling, it is the very first canned wine in BC.

The View's tasting room and winery is housed in Ward's original packinghouse, as is Wards Hard Cider, the other arm of this successful family operation. For many years, Wards Hard Cider was quietly playing second fiddle and serving the local cider lovers—until recently, when a cider renaissance began and it exploded back onto the hip drink scene.

Jennifer's Pinotage Rosé Wine Jelly

When Jennifer Turton-Molgat was growing up, her Nana Turton's sherry jelly with whipped cream was traditionally served on Christmas or New Year's Eve. "Although we found the sherry flavour somewhat potent as children, my brothers, sisters, cousins and I still relished the dessert. With the transition of our family orchard into grapevines and winemaking, it seemed only natural to try Nana's recipe using wine instead of sherry. The View's Pinotage Rosé is one of my personal favourites. Its vivid strawberry notes and mouth-watering acidity make a delicious, flavourful jelly." And it is so darn pretty! This is a make-ahead dish.

Serves 6

1 bottle dry rosé wine (preferably The View's Pinotage Rosé)
2 cups hulled and sliced strawberries
½ tsp pure vanilla
1½ cups berry sugar
2 Tbsp gelatin powder
2 cups cream, whipped
6 whole strawberries, for garnish

Place the rosé wine and sliced strawberries in a bowl and allow to steep for 30 minutes. Strain the wine into a saucepan, reserving the strawberries.

Heat the wine until nearly boiling, then add the vanilla and stir in the sugar until it dissolves. Remove from heat.

In a medium-size bowl, add about ¼ cup of cold water to the gelatin powder to make it bloom, and stir until it has a thick, smooth, paste-like consistency.

Add a third of the hot wine to the gelatin paste and mix until the gelatin is evenly dissolved and no lumps remain. Return this mixture to the pot with the rest of the wine, and whisk.

Divide the sliced strawberries equally into six clear glass serving bowls or large stemless wine glasses, and pour the wine/gelatin mixture overtop. Allow to set in the fridge for at least 3–4 hours, or overnight.

Remove from the fridge 15 minutes before serving and top with whipped cream and a fresh strawberry. Prepare to have your guests tickled pink.

Pair with: The View's Pinotage Rosé. The only one of its kind in North America, it boasts intense aromas of strawberry and cotton candy followed by flavours of pink grapefruit and tart cranberry and a dry, crisp finish. Pinotage Rosé pairs well with poultry; arugula, strawberry and walnut salad; Caprese salad and prosciutto and balsamic flatbread—and it makes great jelly!

Sperling Vineyards

www.sperlingvineyards.com
1405 Pioneer Road, Kelowna

The Sperling family is legendary in the Okanagan, with deep agricultural roots on both sides of the family tree. The Casorso side of the family were pioneers in the Okanagan's farming and winemaking industries, and the Sperling side were innovators when it comes to wine and grapegrowing.

In 1883 Giovanni Casorso came to Canada from Italy with his wife Rosa to work as an agriculturist for the missionaries in Kelowna. Rosa and her son Napoleon Peter (known as Pete) helped establish Kelowna's very first winery, a co-op that preceded Calona Wines. Her sons Charles and Louis also planted vineyards here.

Pete retired in the 1950s, and his daughter Velma and her husband Bert Sperling took over the family farm. Bert and Velma made a bold move: they converted all of the orchards to vineyards. Bert was a director and president of the BC Grapegrowers' Association for many years and played a pivotal role in the growth and development of the grape industry.

Today, the progressive family team has certified organic vineyards and practises biodynamic viticulture. Bert and Velma's daughter, winemaker Ann Sperling, is a great advocate of biodynamic viticulture and a pioneer and educator in this green and natural style of grapegrowing and winemaking. Ann's sister Susan is also involved with the business, as are Susan's husband, daughter and son-in-law.

The vineyards remain high atop the hillsides of beautiful South East Kelowna, and Velma still lives in the family farmhouse below the vineyards where she was born. The wine shop and tasting room are now conveniently located on Pioneer Road, close to the historic Father Pandosy Mission that employed Great-Grandfather Giovanni when he first arrived in Canada.

A trip to the Pioneer Road tasting room property has plenty to offer. Walk the rows of the extraordinary grapevine labyrinth, a dream realized for Velma; learn more about the history of the winery and view historical family photos; and, of course, try a tasting of their biodynamic, organic wine portfolio.

Coronation Grape Streusel Coffee Cake

Bert Sperling was a strong supporter of the grape-breeding program at the Summerland Research and Development Centre, which created varieties like the Sovereign Coronation grape, BC's most famous seedless table grapes. His daughter Susan Richardson developed this delicious recipe to celebrate her dad's hand in creating these grapes.

Serves 8

Streusel:

¾ cup lightly packed brown sugar

½ cup flour

1 tsp ground cinnamon

¼ cup butter

Cake:

½ cup butter, room temperature

1 cup sugar

2 eggs

1 tsp pure vanilla

2 cups flour

1 tsp baking powder

1 tsp baking soda

½ tsp salt

1 cup sour cream or yogurt

2 cups Coronation grapes, fresh or frozen

Whipped cream, to serve

For the Streusel:

Mix together the sugar, flour and cinnamon. Blend in the butter with a fork or pastry blender until the mixture is crumbly. Set aside.

For the Cake:

Preheat the oven to 350°F. Grease a 10-inch springform pan, and set aside.

In the bowl of a stand mixer fitted with the paddle attachment, cream the butter with the sugar until light and fluffy. Beat in the eggs one at a time, then add the vanilla.

In a separate bowl, sift together the dry ingredients. Add to the creamed mixture, then mix in the sour cream.

Spread half of the batter in the prepared pan. Sprinkle with half of the streusel mix, then half of the Coronation grapes. Repeat with the remaining batter, grapes and streusel. For a pretty effect, push some of the grapes into the batter.

Bake until a toothpick inserted in the centre of the cake comes out clean, about 1 hour.

Serve warm with a big dollop of whipped cream.

Pair with: Sperling Vineyards Vidal Icewine. The Vidal grapes were hand-harvested by family and friends in the dead of our Okanagan winter, at -11°C (12°F). The result is a luscious rich wine to be enjoyed with rich cheese or fruit desserts or on its own to bring a new dimension of pleasure to any meal.

Indigenous World Winery

www.indigenousworldwinery.com
2218 Horizon Drive, West Kelowna

Like true Okanagan royalty, the Louie family's deep roots trickle into the very soul of this beautiful region. Proprietors Robert and Bernice Louie both have Okanagan Syilx ancestry, a people that have lived in the Okanagan Valley for thousands of years. Robert was chief of the Westbank First Nation for over 24 years, and the couple met through Bernice's mother, Rose Derrickson, who served as one of Robert's councillors during his leadership. Their creation of a family winery and vineyards is a manifestation of the agricultural future of the community and a great celebration of the Indigenous history of the land.

Located in West Kelowna, Indigenous World Winery is perched on the hillside, looking north to Okanagan Lake. With vineyards on the bench below, the views are mesmerizing. On-site there is a glass-walled tasting room that also offers a wonderful array of handmade Indigenous-themed gifts. Below, the Red Fox Club restaurant, with creative chef Andrea Callan at the helm, is surrounded by a beautifully landscaped lawn. The property also features a stunning authentic teepee, complete with fire pit—a gathering place for many dinners and celebrations, an extraordinary Okanagan experience.

Robert is a lawyer by trade, but his family roots in agriculture have always whispered to him. His grandmother raised cattle and grew hay, and as a young man, Robert worked in the fruit and grape industry. Bernice also has a history in farming, and her father had a cattle ranch. The two wanted to create a legacy in agriculture to leave for their children and to keep them connected to the land. They decided on the wine industry as the most viable option and embarked on their viticulture journey in 2014, beginning with planting 2.5 acres into vines that they used to create their estate label. The family has also entered the distilling business, with an Indigenous World Spirits label underway. Vodka, barrel-aged whisky and gin (that will include secret Indigenous botanicals) are all in the works.

"The land has, since time immemorial, been that of the Okanagan Syilx People," explains Bernice. "Robert inherited 80 acres of land from his stemtema (grandmother) and was born at home on the farmland. The winery production facility is located squarely within a special site of the land that always seemed to have a warm pocket of air in the wintertime and was where the cattle congregated."

Robert and Bernice's children, Trenton and Cassandra, also work in the family winery business and have wines named after their traditional Okanagan Syilx names. Trenton's name, Hee-Hee-Tel-Kin, means "the elusive high-country stag with large antlers"—the Okanagan Syilx People say that a sighting of this mystical animal is a once-in-a-lifetime experience that is remembered forever. Cassandra's name is La'p Cheet, which poetically translates to "the sparkle that shines/glimmers off a high mountain stream."

Roasted Bone Marrow & Bannock

Chef Andrea Callan is the talent behind Indigenous World Winery's on-site restaurant, the Red Fox Club, which highlights local ingredients and Indigenous dishes in a delicious expression of the winery's terroir. Andrea created this recipe in honour of proprietor Bernice Louie's favourite dish. Growing up, Bernice would eat the family's leftover bone marrow—and was eventually given the nickname "Bonehead"! Bannock is a traditional Indigenous fried bread that is served with most meals.

Serves 6

Bannock:

1¼ tsp active dry yeast

4 cups bread flour

1 tsp salt

1 tsp sugar

1 Tbsp canola oil, plus more for frying

Bone Marrow:

6 high-quality beef marrow bones, split lengthwise (see note)

3 Tbsp coarsely chopped herbs, such as rosemary or sage

Salt and pepper

Note: For the marrow bones, tell your butcher that you are roasting them to serve and not using them in stock. You will need half to one bone per person.

For the Bannock:
Line two baking sheets with parchment paper.

In the bowl of a stand mixer fitted with the dough hook, mix the yeast into 2 cups of lukewarm water. Let sit for 5 minutes to activate the yeast, then add the flour, salt, sugar and oil. Start the mixer on low speed and combine until a homogeneous mixture forms.

Let the mixture sit in the bowl and rise at room temperature until it expands to double the size, 40–60 minutes. It will be very soft.

Lightly oil your hands and portion the dough into six equal pieces. Drop the pieces onto the prepared sheets and lightly press down with your fingers to create a uniform height—about 2 inches. Cover the sheets with a slightly damp towel and let proof for 30 minutes.

While the bannock is proofing, preheat the oven to 400°F. Bake the bannock until golden brown, about 20–25 minutes. (Alternatively, if you prefer to fry the bannock, heat some canola oil to 350°F in a deep pan or deep fryer. Drop in pieces of dough and fry until lightly golden, about 3 minutes per side, then drain on paper towel.)

For the Bone Marrow:
Preheat the oven to 400°F. Place the bones on a parchment-lined baking sheet, marrow side up, and season generously with herbs, salt and pepper.

Cook until deep golden and bubbling, about 20–30 minutes. Serve with bannock and a spoon to scrape out the marrow.

Pair with: Indigenous World La'p Cheet Sparkling Rosé. This sparkling wine has aromas of raspberry, blackberry, strawberry and red licorice alongside cherry, cassis and pink grapefruit. The finish is long with a fruity, slightly herbaceous savoury note.

Quails' Gate Winery

www.quailsgate.com
3303 Boucherie Road, West Kelowna

In Okanagan wine country, Quails' Gate Winery is in a category all its own. Located in West Kelowna, with vineyards spilling down the hillside to Okanagan Lake, this property offers one of the most spectacular lake views in the industry.

In addition to the visual delights, the Stewart family has created an authentic winery experience that celebrates the family's heritage as well as that of the Okanagan's farming history. On-site you will find a beautiful tasting room, the vineyard and surrounding gardens, and the multi-award-winning farm-to-table Old Vines Restaurant. The estate also includes the treasured Allison House (circa 1873), a heritage building that was home to one of the region's first pioneers.

Dick Stewart and his wife Rosemary purchased the winery land in 1956 and planted the first vines in 1961. The winery opened its doors in 1989. It was one of the very first farmgate wineries in BC and one of the first wineries in Canada.

The Stewart family are a close-knit clan, and many of them are involved in the winery and the agriculture industry. Dick and Rosemary's children, Ben, Tony, Cynthia (Walker) and Andrea (McFadden), all still reside in Kelowna. Tony is now CEO of the winery, but Ben (and wife Ruth) originally spearheaded the winery operation. Andrea opened the Okanagan Lavender & Herb Farm on a property that originally was part of her grandfather's nursery land.

The future holds exciting plans for more of the Stewarts' legacy farmland. Almost directly across the lake from Quails' Gate, on the slopes of South Kelowna, is a stunning lake-view property that "Poppa" Dick Stewart, Dick's father, once farmed with his brother. Andrea explains. "At over 200 acres, the land provided us with resources to support the growth of our winery. The lone pine in the southwest corner marks the resting place of our grandparents and our uncle and is where our father will eventually rest as well."

Over the next few years, the property will be planted with a focus mainly on white varietals, allowing for some complementary replanting on the Quails' Gate site, whose southern exposure and proximity to the shores of Okanagan Lake have made it one of the best Pinot Noir locations in the Okanagan Valley.

Jan's Cauliflower Soup
with Apple Curry Marshmallows

When Jan Dobbener married into the Stewart family, he happily joined the family business at Quails' Gate Winery. A formally trained chef, he likes to serve this dairy- and gluten-free soup at family gatherings in the fall. For a vegan option, exclude the marshmallows.

Serves 6–8

Apple Curry Marshmallows:

Cornstarch, for dusting

½ cup apple juice

2 Tbsp gelatin powder

2 cups sugar

1 Tbsp glucose syrup or white corn syrup

4 egg whites

1 Tbsp curry powder, plus extra for sprinkling

Soup:

2 Tbsp vegetable oil

2 onions, thinly sliced

1 medium head cauliflower, chopped into small pieces

1 leek (white portion only), diced

4 cloves garlic, minced

½ Tbsp cumin seeds

½ Tbsp curry powder

6 cups vegetable stock

1 (398 ml/14 oz) can coconut milk

Salt and pepper

Olive oil, to drizzle (optional)

Chive blossoms, to garnish (optional)

Nasturtium leaves, to garnish (optional)

For the Apple Curry Marshmallows:

These need 2 hours to set and can be made ahead.

Line an 8 × 10-inch glass or ceramic baking dish with parchment paper and heavily coat it with cornstarch using a fine strainer or sieve. Set aside.

In a small saucepan over medium-high heat, bring ¼ cup of the apple juice to a boil, and stir in the gelatin. Remove from heat and set aside.

In another small saucepan over low heat, warm the rest of the apple juice. Stir in the sugar until it dissolves, then stir in the glucose syrup. Pour into the saucepan with the juice and gelatin and set aside to cool.

In the bowl of a stand mixer fitted with the whisk attachment, beat the egg whites until stiff peaks form. Add the curry powder and whisk until combined. With the mixer running on high speed, slowly add the juice mixture in a thin stream until combined, then turn off the mixer.

Scoop the marshmallow mixture into the prepared pan, levelling with a spatula until even, then finish by coating the top with another thick layer of cornstarch (it is super sticky). Cover with plastic wrap and set aside in a cool, dry place (not the fridge). Allow to set for about 2 hours.

Once the marshmallows have fully set, ensure that they are liberally sprinkled with cornstarch to prevent them from sticking to each other. Slice into 2-inch cubes with a knife dipped in cornstarch, or use a small round biscuit cutter (or the size or shape of your preference). Marshmallows will keep for 3–4 days in the pantry in an airtight container.

continued

For the Soup:

In a large stockpot over medium-low heat, heat the oil. Sauté the onions until translucent, about 5 minutes, then add the cauliflower and sauté for another 2 minutes. Add the leeks and garlic and sauté for another 3–4 minutes, until the leeks have softened, stirring continuously to ensure that they do not brown on the bottom.

Stir in the cumin seeds and curry powder, then pour in the stock. Lower the heat and simmer, covered, until the cauliflower is soft, 20–25 minutes.

Add the coconut milk and salt and pepper to taste. Remove from heat.

With an immersion blender, blend the soup until smooth (or transfer to a blender when slightly cooled).

Strain and serve hot, topped with a fabulous apple curry marshmallow. If you like, sprinkle with curry powder, drizzle with olive oil and garnish with chive blossoms and nasturtium leaves.

Pair with: Quails' Gate Chasselas-Pinot Blanc-Pinot Gris. This beautifully aromatic wine has notes of fresh orchard fruit, gooseberry, lime cordial, spring blossoms and white flowers. Slightly off-dry, the palate is fresh and fruity with balanced acidity and a lovely citrus finish.

Lucy Mary's Lemon Meringue Pie

This Stewart family favourite is from Lucy Mary Whitworth Stewart, lovingly known as Gram. Gram was given the recipe by her sister, Aunt Charlotte Whitworth Springer, who actually holds a delicious slice of Vancouver history as the owner of the famed Bon Ton Café on downtown Granville Street in the 1930s. It is a delicious recipe, and you will feel proud as punch to make a real "from scratch" lemon pie.

Makes 1 (10-inch) pie

1 (10-inch) pie shell (store-bought or recipe on page 150)

Lemon Custard:

5 Tbsp cornstarch

½ tsp salt

⅓ cup lemon juice

2 Tbsp butter

Zest of 1 lemon

1 cup sugar

2 egg yolks, stirred

Meringue:

2 (or 3 if you like higher meringue) egg whites, room temperature

Pinch of salt

4 Tbsp sugar

Blind-bake the pie shell and allow it to cool completely.

For the Lemon Custard:

In a saucepan or double boiler over medium heat, stir the cornstarch and salt in ½ cup of cold water until completely blended. Add 1½ cups of boiling water and cook, stirring, until nice and thick, about 10–15 minutes.

Stir in the lemon juice, butter and lemon zest. Once the butter is melted, stir in the sugar. Whisk in the egg yolks and cook the mixture until it thickens, stirring, about 3 more minutes. Remove from heat and cool (to cool completely refrigerate it, if you like).

When you are ready to bake the pie, preheat the oven to 400°F. Ladle the lemon custard into the cooled pie shell and make the meringue.

For the Meringue:

Place the egg whites in the bowl of a stand mixer fitted with the whisk attachment, and sprinkle with salt. Whip at medium speed, gradually adding the sugar, until stiff peaks form. Spoon on top of the lemon pie, using a spatula to make waves and peaks. Bake until the peaks of the meringue are a light golden brown, about 10–12 minutes. Allow to cool completely before serving.

Thanks, Gram!

Pair with: Quails' Gate Totally Botrytis Affected Optima. Medium lemon in colour, this decadent Sauterne-style dessert wine has a pronounced intensity on the nose. Expect bright notes of peach, apricot, summer blossoms and almonds. On the palate, sweet notes of orange zest and stone fruit are balanced with vibrant acidity and a long citrus finish.

Mission Hill Family Estate Winery

www.missionhillwinery.com
1730 Mission Hill Road, West Kelowna

Sitting like a crown atop the hillside in West Kelowna, Anthony von Mandl's Mission Hill Family Estate Winery symbolizes a dream for the future, a grand talisman for a long and rich history for the BC wine industry. The supreme elegance and old-world European style of the estate was created by renowned architect Tom Kundig, who translated Anthony's vision into design.

Each year, visitors come from around the world to visit the winery and dine at the epic Terrace Restaurant, which offers soaring bird's-eye views of the vineyards and Okanagan Lake below. There is a stunning gift shop and tasting room on the estate, and the opportunity to book private tastings in exclusive rooms, including the gorgeous underground wine cellar. Visitors can join the wine club for access to perks like special dinners and opportunities to buy first-release tickets to concert performances. The winery's

outdoor amphitheatre hosts concerts featuring world-renowned performers. The property is home to some exquisite art pieces from the von Mandl family art collection, including a Chagall tapestry and various sculptures of note. A landmark 12-storey bell tower keeps watch over the estate and is a nostalgic reminder of Anthony's time spent in Europe as a boy—for him, the bells represent a special sense of time and place. Mission Hill Family Estate Winery is a world-class experience on every level.

The face behind the wine at Mission Hill is Aussie Darryl Brooker (pictured here), the charming and knowledgeable president, and also a winemaker. His passion for organic viticulture makes him the perfect leader for the estate as the von Mandl vineyards reach for certified organic status. Darryl explains, "Organic viticulture is very important to me and to our business. We believe that it is so important to protect what we have—and given that we have beautiful, pristine lakes up and down the valley, it is our responsibility to protect the environment. Organic certification is really the first step in developing a fully sustainable agriculture region."

Darryl's love affair with the Okanagan was immediate. "It is the most stunning wine region in the world," he says. "Once here, I could not believe the diversity in soil, climate, elevation and season. I believe we have only just started here in the Okanagan; we now have vine age and a better understanding of our climate, soil and the sub-appellations. The future is very bright."

Darryl's Sesame-Crusted Tuna

Winemaker and president of Mission Hill Family Estate Winery, Darryl Brooker is an Aussie who loves to entertain friends and family outdoors when he is not in the vineyard or cellar. This gorgeous tuna and salad combo is a go-to for Darryl not only because it pairs wonderfully well with a patio under the Australian or Okanagan sun, but also because it is easy to prepare.

Serves 8

Dressing:

⅔ cup crunchy peanut butter

⅓ cup olive oil

3 Tbsp honey

3 Tbsp rice vinegar

1 Tbsp soy sauce

1 Tbsp lime juice

1 Tbsp ground ginger

Salad:

1 head red cabbage, chopped

1 head romaine lettuce, chopped

3 carrots, chopped

1 yellow bell pepper, chopped

⅓ cup chopped cilantro

⅓ cup chopped green onions

1 cup roasted peanuts, chopped

Tuna:

8 (each 6 oz) ahi tuna steaks, 1 inch thick

Salt and pepper

½ cup black sesame seeds

½ cup white sesame seeds

4 Tbsp canola oil

For the Dressing:

In a large bowl, whisk all the dressing ingredients thoroughly to combine. Chill in the fridge for at least 30 minutes.

For the Salad:

Place all the salad ingredients in a bowl and toss. Set aside.

For the Tuna:

Season the tuna steaks with salt and pepper and set aside. In a shallow bowl, mix together the black and white sesame seeds. Working one at a time, dip each seasoned tuna steak into the sesame seeds, coating all the sides evenly, and transfer to a plate to await cooking.

In a large frying pan over high heat, heat the oil. Cooking in batches depending on the size of your frying pan, place the tuna steaks in the pan and cook, uncovered, until the white sesame seeds start to turn golden, about 1 minute. Flip the tuna and continue to cook until both sides are just golden. Remove to a plate and repeat cooking instructions for the remaining steaks.

Transfer the cooked tuna to a cutting board and cut into thick slices. To serve, spread the dressing over a serving dish, then top with the sliced tuna and the salad.

Pair with: Mission Hill Perpetua Chardonnay. Perpetua's rich, creamy texture and finely woven, bright acidity are anchored by pear, lemon curd and baking spice flavours. This wine shows an alluring purity and seamless integration of all the elements, with good length and intensity.

Kalala Organic Estate Winery

www.kalala.ca
3361 Glencoe Road, West Kelowna

You will find very good karma at Kalala Organic Estate Winery. With a manifesto that reads "In pursuit of harmony," owner Karnail Singh Sidhu's story is a wonderful one of honest success. When he arrived in Canada with an engineering degree and was unable to find employment in his field, he took a job in a vineyard. This would become his destiny, as the art of viticulture and organic agriculture captured his heart.

He named his winery Kalala, after the small village in India where he was raised. His grandparents told him the legend of how the village came to be: Long ago, in northern India, farmers working in the beautiful and distant flatlands came upon a wolf and lamb sitting peacefully together. They found this coexistence so inspiring that they moved their village to this very spot in hopes that the same harmony would be reflected in the village, and they named it Kalala, meaning "Miracle Place."

Creating organic vineyards is not a miracle, but becoming certified organic does take time and absolute dedication. Kalala's vineyards surround the winery, which is located on the upper bench of West Kelowna. Away from the main winery area, Karnail has forged his own micro region of organic land in a farm and orchard district. The winery has a picnic area where visitors can sit to meditate and absorb the organic air, and it is large enough to host events. The tasting room is lined with medals, and one in particular stands out: the number-one Chardonnay icewine in the world at the Chardonnay du Monde competition in France. This prestigious competition could be described as the Olympics of winemaking.

This is a family operation. Karnail's wife Narinder is involved on the business side, and their two daughters, Simran and Kiran, participate when they can. The wonderful vibe here is an extension of Karnail's kind and gentle personality—it feels like the land itself exudes happiness from the loving care it has been given. As a leader in the organic farming movement and a sought-after viticulture consultant, Karnail shares his knowledge with all those interested in organics. He also produces a second line of small-batch premium wines called Dostana, which means "friendship" in Hindi.

Karnail has built a wonderful team at the winery. Winemaker Tibor (Tibby) Erdelyi has been with Karnail since 2008 and is meticulous about his craft—not surprising, as he, like many winemakers, has a background as a chef. Ethnically Hungarian, Tibby came to Canada from Serbia in 1989. After many years behind the pans at fine restaurants in Vancouver, he became absorbed in his passion for winemaking and organics.

Tibby's Hungarian Harvest Goulash

Kalala winemaker Tibor (Tibby) Erdelyi grew up with the delicious flavours of Hungary and Serbia. He's also a trained chef, but this recipe is one he was taught by his mome and grandmome. This rich and hearty stew is a wonderful way to warm your bones after a day spent harvesting in the vineyard. Tibby likes to splurge on tenderloin tips, but you can also use chuck stewing beef.

Serves 6

3 strips bacon, diced (see note)

2 yellow onions, sliced

2 sweet yellow banana peppers or 1 yellow bell pepper, sliced

2 lb stewing beef, cut into 1½-inch cubes

2 beefsteak tomatoes, diced (or 3 cups chopped canned tomatoes)

3 cloves garlic, minced

1 tsp caraway seeds

1 tsp salt

½ tsp pepper

1½ lb yellow potatoes, cubed

¼ cup Hungarian paprika (see note)

1 large bay leaf

Buttered bread, to serve

Notes: If you don't have bacon on hand, you can substitute 2–3 Tbsp butter, melting it in the Dutch oven before adding the onions and peppers. The traditional option is pork fat, which falls somewhere in between.

There are many different types of Hungarian paprika, and they will all work well. Hot paprika is very hot! Use it for up to ¼ of the total paprika, blended with another type.

In a large Dutch oven over medium-high heat, fry the bacon.

Add the onions and peppers and cook until golden brown. Add the beef cubes, tomatoes, garlic, caraway seeds, salt and pepper, and cook until the tomatoes begin to brown slightly, about 15–20 minutes. Add the potatoes, paprika, bay leaf and enough water to cover the mixture by ½ inch (about 3 cups of water, depending on your Dutch oven).

Bring the mixture to a boil, then cover, lower the heat and simmer until the meat is tender, about 45 minutes. Adjust seasoning if needed. Serve with thick slices of buttered bread.

Pair with: Kalala Gewürztraminer. On the nose, enjoy tropical notes of mango, pineapple, passion fruit and lychee. On the palate you will find flavours of anise, cloves and cinnamon.

View of Naramata Bench from Bench 1775 Winery

Okanagan
South

Peachland & Summerland

Penticton & Naramata

Okanagan Falls

Introduction

Okanagan South is a series of charming townships. Peachland, Summerland, Penticton, Naramata and Okanagan Falls are each loaded with their own unique beauty, personality, spectacular views and, of course, fantastic wines!

As you wind your way south, along the lakeshore from West Kelowna, you first drive through Peachland and then on to Summerland. Still small, but growing, Summerland is an agriculture-rich lakeside village that is becoming known for its wine production. Bottleneck Drive, which snakes its way up into the hillside, is a wine tour already set for visitors.

Continuing on, you'll reach the small city of Penticton and its super-glamorous extension Naramata, where you will truly experience the wow of wine country. Naramata is on a "bench" (an area of flatter land between slopes). Perched above the sandy cliffs over the lake and slowly sloping up to the mountains behind, Naramata Bench provides the perfect conditions for growing grapes. It has over 40 wineries packed into its beautiful landscape and has become a full-on international wine destination. Naramata village proper is on the lake near the end of the long and winding Naramata Road. The journey into the area is totally green, with orchards and vineyards along the bench and soaring views down Okanagan Lake from most of the properties.

Coming out the other side of Penticton, you will soon arrive at the unassuming little town of Okanagan Falls. Don't be fooled by this micro town centre—the hills surrounding it are rich with some of the best wineries the Okanagan has to offer. In recent years Okanagan Falls has become a sub-appellation, marking its distinctive range of terroir.

Fitzpatrick Family Vineyards

www.fitzwine.com
697 Highway 97 South, Peachland

Fancy a little bubbly by the lake? Driving along the lakeside highway between Summerland and Peachland proper, a great arch of an entrance marked "Greata Ranch" will catch your eye. Turn off and follow the vineyard-lined driveway toward Okanagan Lake, and it will guide you to the beautiful Sparkling Bar and the Bistro at Fitzpatrick Family Vineyards. Plan to stay a while.

This unique lakefront setting features 40 acres of vines separated into 12 smaller, carefully tended blocks, offering a distinctive terroir to the winemaking program. The winery produces both sparkling and still wines, with a focus on what grows best here: traditional-method sparkling wine, crisp whites and elegant, focused reds.

Ross Fitzpatrick clearly remembers visiting a stunning 130-acre orchard in Summerland as a child in the 1940s. Specializing in peaches, pears and cherries, it was called Greata Ranch. When Ross grew up and went away to school, those warm memories of the Okanagan farmland and agriculture industry lured him back. In 1986 he purchased Uniacke Winery in the Mission area of Kelowna, which would become the landmark CedarCreek Estate Winery. His son Gordon joined the family business in 1996 as president and ran the winery until they sold in 2014.

While he was operating CedarCreek, Ross fulfilled a dream and purchased that beautiful peach orchard in Summerland. After selling CedarCreek, he and Gordon spent the next few years restoring Greata Ranch, planting vines and waiting for their next winery vision to unfold. As it turns out, it was a sparkling one. Fitzpatrick Family Vineyards opened in 2017 with a colourful new label and branding. "Through winemaking, education and hospitality, we bring a little more sparkle into daily life in a way that is approachable, cultivated, effervescent, celebratory and detailed," says Gordon. The star shape on the label is inspired by the famous quote attributed to Dom Pérignon: "Come quickly, I am tasting the stars."

Dungeness Crab, Spring Peas & Garlic Noodles

This is one of the Fitzpatrick family's favourite celebration dishes, a recipe created by former bistro chef Jeremy Tucker. Featuring BC Dungeness crab and tender spring peas, it is delicious and pairs perfectly with Fitz sparkling wine!

Serves 4

1 lb fresh pasta noodles, such as linguini

4 Tbsp olive oil

3 cloves garlic, minced

4 Tbsp butter

½ cup shelled spring peas

2½ tsp oyster sauce

1 tsp chicken bouillon

8 oz Dungeness crabmeat

½ cup chopped flat-leaf parsley

Parmesan cheese, to serve

Pea shoots, to serve

Cook the pasta according to the package directions. Strain and set aside.

In a large pan over low heat, heat the olive oil. Sauté the garlic for a minute, then add the butter and peas. Stir in the oyster sauce and chicken bouillon and cook until the peas are tender, 3–5 minutes. Add the noodles to the pan and toss well.

Divide the noodles between four bowls, top with the crabmeat and parsley, and garnish with Parmesan cheese and pea shoots. Serve immediately.

Cheers!

Pair with: Fitz Brut, the Fitzpatrick family's signature cuvée. Similar to the grower Champagnes of France, their approach involves adjusting the blend percentages from vintage to vintage, striving to evoke a clear statement on the year, terroir and people who contributed to the wine's development.

Silkscarf Winery

www.silkscarf-winery.com
4917 Gartrell Road, Summerland

While meandering along the scenic Bottleneck Drive in Summerland, you will find Silkscarf, owned and operated by the Manoff family. What makes this boutique winery so special, besides the fantastic wine, is that the wine shop is connected to the family home. "Over the years, our daily lives and family traditions have become interwoven with the cycles and rhythms of the vineyard, making this generous piece of land a true home for us," says Roie Manoff. And you will feel at home too—especially in the summer months, when you can sit with a glass or bottle of wine on the patio, enjoying their hospitality and the spectacular lake view.

You will probably find Roie in the tasting room, and with his warm smile and deep knowledge about his wines and the industry, he is a delight to visit with. Roie spent 26 years in the Israeli Air Force as a fighter pilot. The winery's name is a tribute to the first Israeli pilots, who flew in open-air cockpits, their colourful silk scarves flying in the wind.

Roie and his wife Ruth discovered Summerland while they were travelling, and they fell in love with the area. They purchased the apple orchard that would become Silkscarf's vineyard in 2004, and the winery has been their retirement project. They grow a range of varieties on the over 10-acre estate, including Gewürztraminer, Viognier, Chardonnay, Riesling, Pinot Gris, Cabernet Sauvignon, Merlot, Pinot Noir, Malbec and Syrah.

Winemaking is a collaborative family effort here. Roie and his son Idan (who is also the vineyard manager) are the official winemakers, but every member of the family (Ruth, Ateret, Itamar, Einat), each with their own unique and talented nose and palate, is involved in tasting the wine at different stages—especially when it's time to approve for bottling. They all participate in tasting, tweaking and retasting until everyone is pleased with the outcome.

Philosophy discussions go on in the cellar here—especially between Idan and his partner, Ateret. "The art of winemaking is a sensory experience, like cooking," says Ateret. "And it is very emotional."

Silkscarf's Upside-Down Grape-Leaf Rice

Many years ago, Ateret Buchman operated a tiny eatery at Silkscarf Winery, where she offered incredible Mediterranean-Israeli-inspired cuisine that locals are still buzzing about. She and Ruth Manoff developed this stunning dish—its dramatic presentation makes it a showstopper at dinner parties.

"This is an all-time favourite recipe of our family that can easily accompany many different meals," says Ateret. "We often prepare it as a side, and have experimented with many variations over the years. This is the basic and most loved version, and it's both vegan and gluten-free."

Serves 6

Rice:

2½ cups basmati rice

10–20 fresh (or preserved) grape leaves (enough to line the pot)

3 Tbsp olive oil

1½ tsp salt

1½ tsp ground turmeric

½ tsp ground coriander

Pinch of white pepper

Topping:

6 dried figs

¼ cup dried goji berries or cranberries

¼ cup pine nuts

2 Tbsp olive oil

1 onion, thinly sliced

1 carrot, julienned

¼ cup raisins

Pinch of ground cinnamon

Pinch of ground cumin

3 Tbsp maple syrup

For the Rice:

Wash the rice under running water until the water runs clear, then set it aside to drain. Bring a pot of salted water to a boil and blanch the fresh grape leaves until they change colour to dark green, just a few seconds. Transfer to ice water to stop the cooking process, then drain. If you are using preserved leaves, separate them and soak in cold water for 30 minutes, then drain.

Grease a medium-size nonstick pot with 2 Tbsp of the olive oil (the pot size will determine the size of your finished dish). Line the bottom and sides with overlapping grape leaves, going high enough up the sides that all the rice will be covered when added.

In a small bowl, mix the rice with the salt, turmeric, coriander, pepper and the remaining olive oil. Add the mixture to the leaf-lined pot. Pour in 4 cups of water (or the amount suggested on the rice package) and stir gently to mix, being careful not to displace the leaves.

Bring the mixture to a boil over high heat, then turn down the heat to low and cover until the rice is fully cooked, about 20 minutes. Allow to rest, covered, for 10–15 minutes, or keep warm in a 160°F oven until ready to serve.

For the Topping:
While the rice is cooking, boil 4 cups of water. Remove from the heat and soak the figs and goji berries in the water for 5 minutes, then drain. Slice the figs.

In a dry frying pan over medium heat, toast the pine nuts, stirring regularly, until they become fragrant and start to brown. Remove to a bowl and set aside.

In the same frying pan over medium-high heat, heat the olive oil and stir-fry the onions until they start to turn golden. Add the carrots, continuing to stir for another minute or so. Add the figs, goji berries, toasted pine nuts, raisins, cinnamon, cumin and maple syrup, and stir for another minute or so. Add 2 Tbsp of water, stir, turn the heat to low and cover the frying pan. Allow the mixture to steam for a couple of minutes, then remove from heat. Remove the lid and allow the mixture to cool to room temperature.

To serve, fold the tips of the grape leaves overtop the cooked rice, then carefully flip the rice onto a serving plate. It is easiest to hold a plate onto the top of the pot and then invert it directly onto the plate. Spoon the topping on top and slice as you would a cake.

Pair with: Silkscarf Viognier. Pale lemon in colour, it exhibits a fresh and fragrant nose of apricot, white peach, grapefruit, Granny Smith apple and crushed rocks. The palate is dry, showing a typical creaminess that is nicely balanced by bright acidity and flavours of apricot, grapefruit and chamomile.

8th Generation Vineyard

www.8thgeneration.com
6807 Highway 97, Summerland

As proudly decreed on the side of the winery building, 8th Generation Vineyard brings Okanagan wine lovers over 235 years of European winemaking history—and counting. This family's impressive lineage in old-world wines and vines far exceeds the history of our BC and Canadian wine industry.

Bernd and Stefanie Schales are an example of the old world re-rooting in the new world. Winemaking has been a continuous tradition in their family for eight generations, originating in Germany. Bernd's ancestor Christian Schales planted his first grapes in 1783 in the small Rheinhessen village of Dalsheim, and Stefanie is actually a 10th-generation grapegrower. Stefanie and Bernd grew up in the wine industry in Germany, and met at—you guessed it!—a wine festival. They married and started a family there, and then decided to leave Germany in 2003 to build the first-generation Schales winery on Canadian soil.

"The Okanagan is the ideal terroir to grow fruit-driven whites with a realistic acidity, plus wonderful bold reds," explains Stefanie. "It is small and will always be boutique compared to other wine regions. There is no better place than Canada, as this was not just about growing grapes and making wine—it was also a family move with our one-year-old daughter." The couple now has three kids: Johanna, Philipp and Helena, and they are a busy bunch in perpetual motion.

Located just off the highway in Summerland, the winery's beautiful, modern tasting room is in a little renovated house surrounded by the vineyard. There is a picnic area to sip wine and linger, and snacks available to purchase on-site.

With 20 acres of grape production spread between Okanagan Falls, Summerland and Naramata, 8th Generation has a wonderful range of terroir to create their portfolio from. The goal is to craft fruit-driven, balanced wines with a crisp acidity. "Our wines speak about the terroir as well as the winemakers' heritage," says Stefanie.

They are making both whites and reds and are well loved for their two varieties of frizzante: Integrity and Confidence. In 2008 they started a movement with their capped prosecco-style frizzante wines—the more casual, cost-efficient sibling of sparkling wine—starting with a straight 100% Chardonnay frizzante. "Quite a landslide we created with that in the Okanagan wine scene," Stefanie says.

Pair with: 8th Generation Integrity Frizzante. This delightful, versatile wine is a sparkling blend of Chardonnay, Pinot Gris and Kerner. Notes of apricot and pear combine with a soft citrus on the nose; the palate explodes with honey, pineapple, honeydew melon and more soft exotic fruit.

Zwiebelkuchen

Onion Quiche

This quiche is a Schales family tradition, served to celebrate the first crush of grapes after harvest and bless the new vintage. Stefanie Schales serves it to her family and crew in the 8th Generation wine cellar, paired with a glass of *neuer wein* (new wine, fresh from the tank of fermenting white wine). The sweet, cloudy, bubbly wine pairs perfectly with the onions and bacon in this recipe. Ask your local winery if you can purchase a jug of neuer wein to pair with your own zwiebelkuchen.

Serves 6

Dough:

4 tsp active dry yeast

½ cup + 5 Tbsp warm milk

Pinch of sugar

2 cups flour

1 egg

¼ cup butter

½ tsp salt

Filling:

3 Tbsp canola oil

6 cups finely chopped sweet onions (about 5 large)

3 slices Schinkenspeck or good bacon, finely chopped

1 cup sour cream

2 eggs

½ tsp caraway seeds

½ tsp salt

1 Tbsp flour

For the Dough:

In a small bowl, mix the yeast with 5 Tbsp of the warm milk, add the sugar and leave in a warm spot to rise until frothy, about 5 minutes.

In the bowl of a stand mixer fitted with the dough hook, place the flour, egg, butter, salt, the rest of the milk and the yeast mixture. Start the mixer on low speed, and mix until one big ball of dough has formed, at least 5 minutes. If the dough is too wet or dry, add additional flour or milk to adjust—it should be elastic and not too sticky.

Cover the dough with a clean tea towel and leave to rest in a warm spot until it has doubled in size, about 1 hour.

For the Filling:

In the meantime, in a large frying pan over low heat, heat the oil. Sauté the onions until they are soft but not brown, about 20 minutes. Add the Schinkenspeck, remove from heat and set aside to cool (it will cook in the oven later).

In a bowl, whisk together the sour cream, eggs, caraway seeds and salt. Sprinkle the flour over the onion mixture, add the egg mixture and stir it all together with a wooden spoon.

Preheat the oven to 350°F and grease a pan or line it with parchment. Ideally, use a 15-inch deep-dish pizza pan. Transfer the dough to a lightly floured surface and roll it out to fit the shape of your pan, with an additional 2 inches of dough on all edges. Lay it out on the pan, creating a 2-inch-high "curb" around the edges to contain the filling.

Using a spatula, spread the filling over the dough. Bake until the crust is crispy and golden brown, about 45 minutes. Cool and cut into wedges. Prost!

TIME Winery & Evolve Cellars

www.timewinery.com
www.evolvecellars.com
361 Martin Street, Penticton

It's about TIME. Known by many as the godfather of the Okanagan wine industry, Harry McWatters created a number of amazing brands in the Okanagan. He came full circle and welcomed wine lovers to his newest winery, TIME, in 2018. TIME Winery is housed in Penticton's revitalized heritage movie theatre—the first urban winery in the area, with an apropos location and clever name from a man who has invested so much time in the industry and the wine community as a leader, a teacher and a friend.

Despite its status as a heritage building, TIME's design is state of the art, with crisp lines and lofty wood-lined ceilings. Harry's daughter, Christa-Lee McWatters, was with him every step of the way. She is thoroughly educated, with experience in every area of the industry. She is director of marketing for Encore Vineyards Ltd., which encompasses all of their wine labels (McWatters Collection, TIME Winery and Evolve Cellars, which now shares the TIME Winery building) as well as their two restaurants and consulting arm.

Harry's story needs its own novel to do it (and him) justice. He began his involvement in the BC wine industry in 1968 as a sales manager at Casabello Wines in Vancouver. He moved to the Okanagan in 1977 with his family, founding Sumac Ridge Estate Winery in 1980 and See Ya Later Ranch in 1995. He drove the agenda to create a quality wine measuring system known as VQA (Vintners Quality Alliance) in 1990, implementing rules and guidelines to guarantee consumers that they were purchasing BC wine made with local grapes.

"I personally believe that without the introduction of VQA, we would likely not have a wine industry in British Columbia today, and most certainly not the thriving enterprise as we know it," Harry said.

Harry was presented with the Vancouver International Wine Festival's coveted Spirited Industry Professional award in 2017, hailing him as the Okanagan Valley's great wine pioneer and a 50-vintage veteran of the industry. In 2003 Harry received the prestigious Order of British Columbia for his services to the BC wine industry. Harry passed away in July 2019, leaving behind him an extraordinary legacy in the Okanagan wine industry.

Muriel's Stout & Beef Pot Pie

Harry McWatters's mother, Muriel Duke, made this Irish dish for him when he was growing up. Over the years, he altered it slightly, but it is still the ultimate comfort food for his family. "This is our go-to favourite on a cold day," said Harry. "Leftovers are great and it freezes well. It invites more wine to be consumed, too." Harry suggested serving this with a side of green beans.

Serves 4

2 Tbsp flour

Pinch of salt and pepper

2 lb trimmed top sirloin steak, cut into 1-inch cubes

2 Tbsp butter

2 medium onions, peeled and roughly chopped

1 large (473 ml) can stout beer (like Naramata Nut Brown ale)

1 tsp grainy mustard

2 cups quartered mushrooms

1 sheet frozen puff pastry, defrosted

Milk, for brushing

Note: You will need four individual 12 oz ramekins for this recipe.

Preheat the oven to 350°F.

Mix the flour, salt and pepper together in a bowl, then toss the cubes of steak in the mixture until lightly coated.

In a large frying pan over medium-high heat, melt half the butter and lightly brown the meat all over (you may need to do this in two batches). Transfer the meat to an oven-safe dish with a lid (the old-fashioned enamel kind works well).

Add the remaining butter to the frying pan and cook the onions until they are just changing colour, about 4–5 minutes. Spoon the onions over the beef. Deglaze the frying pan with the beer, and pour the liquid over the onions and meat. Cook in the oven, covered, until the beef is very tender (at least 2 hours).

Remove the dish from the oven and stir in the grainy mustard and then the mushrooms. Return to the oven for 30 minutes, then remove. Increase the oven temperature to the heat level recommended on the puff pastry package.

Roll out the puff pastry sheet, then cut into circles the same size as your ramekins (a biscuit cutter or water glass works). Arrange them on a baking sheet lined with parchment paper, and brush with milk. Bake according to package instructions until golden brown.

To serve, add the stew to the ramekins and top each with a pastry round.

Pair with: McWatters Collection Meritage. This bold, elegant wine boasts velvety tannins, well-balanced fruit and oak characteristics. Expect blackberry and cassis with a supple texture. This Meritage is crafted with 50% Cabernet Sauvignon, 35% Merlot and 15% Cabernet Franc, and matured in small French oak casks for 15 months.

Upper Bench Winery & Creamery

www.upperbench.ca
170 Upper Bench Road South, Penticton

Wine + cheese + love = Upper Bench Winery & Creamery. Artisans Gavin and Shana Miller met many years ago on the Naramata Bench, back when they were each embarking on their careers. He is a winemaker originally from the UK, and she is a cheesemaker originally from Nova Scotia. They married and followed both their passions by opening their own winery and creamery.

Wine country in Penticton begins as you leave the city and head toward Naramata on Upper Bench Road, and Upper Bench Winery & Creamery is one of the first wineries you will meet. This farmgate-style facility is decorated with fun murals of wine and cheese painted by a local artist. How could you possibly resist making a stop?

The tasting room here is also a cheese shop, offering visitors a selection of Shana's cheeses alongside Gavin's handcrafted wines, with pairings suggested on the wall. If you want more of this in your life, join the country's only wine and cheese subscription club. Members of the Curds & Corks Club receive a quarterly delivery of six bottles of Upper Bench wine and three perfectly paired cheeses.

There are so many moving parts to this busy family operation. Cheesemaking and winemaking are both happening in different areas of the same building. There is a window into the cheesemaking area where you can watch Shana creating her beautiful cheeses, decked out in her apron, hairnet and trademark pink rubber boots. Off to the side of the wine and cheese shop, you will find their busy seasonal patio restaurant, The Oven, which serves amazing wood-fired pizza—and, of course, wine and cheese plates. The patio backs onto the working vineyard, where you can watch the action ringside, including the antics of their two very busy border collies. It is so fun to just hang out, eat and sip wine while feeling like you are part of the action.

Gavin has a long and celebrated career in the wine industry. His Upper Bench Estate vineyard grows seven varietals on seven acres of meticulously farmed land, all without the use of chemicals or pesticides. Shana, too, uses high-quality local ingredients—in her case, 100% pasteurized Canadian cow's milk from D Dutchmen Dairy in Sicamous, BC—to craft five different washed-rind, Brie and blue cheeses. Like Gavin, she puts so much love into her craft. She even talks to her cheeses—like some gardeners do with their plants—and feels that they taste better when they are happy.

Pair with: Upper Bench Merlot. This smooth, easy-drinking Merlot is full of flavour. On the nose, it displays black cherry, menthol, cassis, spice box, blackberry and anise. On the palate is a perfectly balanced blend of cassis, molasses, coffee, cacao, toasted almonds and cherry.

Upper Bench Cheesy Pizza

Shana and Gavin Miller have always loved to cook at home with their two kids, and pizza has long been a favourite food. That's why they created the beautiful wood-fired pizza oven at their seasonal patio eatery, The Oven, at Upper Bench Winery & Creamery. Former pizza maestro at The Oven, Daniel Johansson, shared this delicious pizza dough recipe with toppings from one of the house specials, featuring—you guessed it—cheese!

Makes 2 large pizza dough balls and topping for 1 pizza

Pizza Dough:

1½ tsp active dry yeast

1 Tbsp sea salt

1½ tsp olive oil

3¾ cups Italian "00" flour

¼ cup whole-wheat flour

Pizza:

Olive oil, for brushing

1 ball pizza dough (recipe above)

1 basil leaf

2 oz Upper Bench U&Brie cheese, sliced

2 oz Upper Bench Gold cheese, sliced

2 oz Upper Bench Okanagan Sun cheese, sliced

Handful of arugula

Maldon sea salt and pepper

Drizzle of lemon olive oil (see note)

Notes: If you don't have lemon olive oil, substitute a squeeze of lemon and a drizzle of good olive oil. The toppings are scaled for one pizza—feel free to multiply as needed!

For the Pizza Dough:

In a small bowl, stir the yeast into ¼ cup of warm water. Let sit for 5 minutes to activate.

In the bowl of a stand mixer fitted with the dough hook, combine 1¼ cups of warm water with the salt and olive oil and gently stir until all the salt has dissolved. Add the activated yeast water to the mixing bowl.

Blend at low speed and gradually add the flours until the mixture comes together into a ball. The dough should be soft, flexible and not too sticky, or too elastic. Depending on the water and flour, this should take about 5–7 minutes.

Using your hands, knead and shape the dough into a ball on the counter to get a smooth skin. Return it to the bowl, cover with a damp cloth and leave for at least 2 hours.

Remove the dough from the bowl and shape into two balls. Wrap the balls in plastic wrap and let sit for 6–8 hours on the counter (the dough also freezes well).

For the Pizza:

Preheat the oven to 550°F. Prepare a pizza stone or baking sheet by brushing with olive oil.

On the prepared pizza stone or baking sheet, form the pizza ball into a disc, using your fingers to press it into shape. Brush on some olive oil, using the basil leaf to spread the oil around, then lay the cheese slices evenly over the pizza.

Bake until the crust is golden brown and the cheese is all melted and bubbly, about 8–12 minutes, rotating the pizza stone or baking sheet halfway through for even cooking.

Remove from the oven and top with arugula, Maldon sea salt, pepper and a drizzle of lemon olive oil.

Roche Wines

www.rterroir.ca
60 Upper Bench Road South, Penticton

Pénélope Furt, a sixth-generation winemaker from Bordeaux, met her perfect pairing in Dylan Roche, a winemaker from Vancouver, over a tankful of grapes on a winemaking sabbatical in New Zealand. "I was working for a small family winery, and he came by one day to drop off a mutual friend. I was head to toe in a tankful of grapes, but I heard him speaking French . . . and the rest is history!"

In 2011 they arrived in the Okanagan with two young children in tow. They opened Roche Wines, their new winery and tasting room, in Penticton in 2017. The modern, sloped-roof winery's large double red doors give it a chic French feel, and the structure just seems to melt into the land.

Pénélope and Dylan are true vignerons, crafting their wines from vine to bottle. "Dylan and I learned winemaking in France, where traditions are very important, and I'm thankful for the knowledge that my family has passed down to me over the centuries," Pénélope says. Pénélope hails from generations of winemakers at Château Les Carmes Haut-Brion, a legendary wine estate in Bordeaux. It was taken over by the state during the French Revolution, then sold in 1840 to Léon Colin, a Bordeaux wine merchant and ancestor of the Chantecailles. The Chantecaille-Furt family owned and managed the estate for generations, until quite recently.

So how did the couple get to the Okanagan? "When my family sold the family estate at the end of 2010, it was a big change for us," recalls Pénélope. "I was in charge of the winemaking, the vine growing, and sales and marketing, and Dylan was working at a winery in Margaux. After some time to think, the decision to move here was clear. Dylan is from North Vancouver, and he grew up coming to the Okanagan every summer to the family cabin. We visited many times and loved the wine region, so we put everything in a container and moved to Penticton. We both feel very happy to be here in the valley."

The Roche family has built their dream winery and family home on their Penticton vineyard, and are happily raising their three children, Eugene, Eileen and Gabriel. They are vignerons, tending their vines and making their own wine.

Boeuf Carottes Facile

Easy Beef & Carrot Stew

Simple and delicious, this rich and tangy stew was a favourite of Pénélope Roche's grand-mère, who made it regularly at their château in Bordeaux. Perfect for a cool evening after a long day of harvesting, this dish, Pénélope says, is like the Bordeaux version of beef bourguignon.

Serves 4–6

2 Tbsp butter

3 lb chuck stewing beef, cut into 1-inch cubes

1½ medium onions, diced

1 tsp garlic powder

Salt and pepper

1½ cups good white wine

1 Tbsp tomato paste

1 cube beef bouillon

1½ lb carrots, sliced

Flat-leaf parsley, to garnish

In a cocotte or Dutch oven over medium-high heat, melt the butter. Add the meat and cook until brown on all sides. Add the onions, garlic powder, salt and pepper and cook until the onions are translucent, about 5 minutes. Deglaze with the white wine, scraping the bottom of the dish.

Add the tomato paste and stir well to combine. Crumble the bouillon cube into the pot and add ¼ cup water.

Cover and cook for 1 hour 15 minutes, then add the carrots and cook for another 45 minutes. Garnish with parsley and serve hot with a side of crusty French bread.

Bon appétit!

Pair with: Roche "Tradition" Pinot Noir. The nose reveals a hint of subtle oak spice, followed by small red berries and cassis. This Pinot Noir's growing complexity has a hint of sous-bois (forest floor). On the palate, sweet but restrained fruit leads to fine tannins and a poised finish.

Poplar Grove Winery

www.poplargrove.ca
425 Middle Bench Road North, Penticton

Poplar Grove Winery owner Dr. Tony Holler is a man of innovation with a thirst for knowledge (and wine!). He, his wife Barbara and their sons are operators of this wine brand and destination winery set on the hillside above Penticton. Stay tuned for news of their boutique hotel opening next door to expand the experience.

There is a restaurant on site, located off the spectacular window-walled tasting room at Poplar Grove, which offers unbeatable views of Okanagan Lake and the city below. Dining by night, guests can admire the sparkling lights from Penticton and Naramata and observe the lit-up communities dotting the enormous lake as it winds north to Kelowna and beyond. The winery is available as a venue for weddings and events.

Tony's entrance into the wine industry was not a whim, but a return to his farming roots in the Okanagan soil. He was born and raised with his seven siblings in Summerland. From tiny Summerland, Tony went off to university in Vancouver, became a doctor and made medical history by discovering the flu vaccine through his pharmaceutical company. He and Barb met while he was a student doctor at Vancouver General and she was a young pediatric nurse.

Tony and Barb's original plan was to build a vacation home on the lake in Naramata for their family to enjoy. But when Poplar Grove Winery came up for sale, they decided to take the plunge.

Their four sons are now all involved in the family wine business. Christopher, Andrew, Matthew and Eric have each taken on different roles in this large operation, which includes Poplar Grove, Monster Vineyards and other vineyards in the south. Tony and Barb raised their children with a strong belief in the value of hard work. Each son has "done time" in the vineyard, learning the business from the roots up, and they have invested in their own vineyards.

Barb shares the family philosophy for success in the wine industry: "Time, talent and energy in the vineyards. If you don't put that time in, it doesn't show in the bottle. You must be master of your own destiny, from vine to bottle." Cheers to that.

Rose's Hubbard Squash Chiffon Pie

So much better than pumpkin pie, this light and delicious pie recipe is a Holler family favourite that was passed down in Barb's family from her Grandma Rose. Hubbard squash are so hard that they are nearly impossible to cut, so Barb's grandmother used to tie them up in a pillowcase and throw them down the stairs to crack them! Barb uses a similar trick with a plastic bag.

Makes 1 (9-inch) pie

1 Hubbard squash, peeled and cut into small cubes
1 cup sugar
1 Tbsp flour
1 tsp ground ginger
1 tsp ground cinnamon
½ tsp mace
Pinch of ground nutmeg
¼ tsp salt
3 eggs, separated
½ cup milk
1 (9-inch) pie shell (store-bought or recipe on page 150)
Whipped cream, to serve
Grand Marnier, to serve (optional)

Preheat the oven to 350°F.

Fill a large saucepan with water and bring to a boil. Add the squash and simmer until fork-tender, 15–20 minutes. Drain and transfer to a blender to purée. Set aside a 1½-cup portion for the pie; you can portion and freeze the rest for future pie making.

In a large bowl, mix together the 1½ cups puréed squash, sugar, flour, spices and salt. In another bowl, beat the egg yolks, then stir in the milk. Add to the squash mixture.

In a separate mixing bowl, beat the egg whites until stiff peaks form. Fold into the squash mixture.

Pour the filling into the pie shell and bake until a knife inserted into the centre of the pie comes out clean, 35–45 minutes.

Serve with a big dollop of whipped cream. If you like, stir a splash of Grand Marnier into the cream while whipping for a special touch.

Pair with: Poplar Grove Late Harvest Viognier. This vibrant wine appears straw-yellow upon first pour. Elements of ripe lychee and jasmine waft to the nose. Boasting flavours of peaches, tangerines and warm baked pear, the wine has a crisp acidity and a complex round mouthfeel.

La Frenz Winery

www.lafrenzwinery.com
1525 Randolph Road, Penticton

La Frenz Winery is a great success story in the BC wine industry, and one of the first wineries you will reach on the illustrious Naramata Bench. Fun fact: the view from its tasting room was depicted on the Canadian $100 bill from 1954 to 1974! Obviously, this is testament to the extraordinarily beautiful vineyard, which overlooks Okanagan Lake and just happens to produce some of the finest wines in the valley.

Owner and winemaker Jeff Martin's inspired passion for sustainable vineyard practices is a model for creating great wines from the soil up. His vision has always included working closely with Mother Nature—he started by building a sustainable ecosystem on his land in the old-fashioned way, using animals and concentrating on the unique conditions of the terroir. "It's about creating diversity in our vineyard monocultures," Jeff says. "Many farmers compensate by adding fertilizers and nutrients, when nature and natural processes do a much better job of it." Jeff's deep knowledge of the Okanagan land and terroir is remarkable—ask him about anything and everything to do with Okanagan wine.

Jeff and his wife Niva were both born and bred in Griffith, New South Wales, Australia, a significant agricultural area. Jeff cut his teeth in the wine industry at the age of 18, working as a trainee winemaker at McWilliam's, a renowned Australian winery that produces half a million cases in their Beelbangera facility. In 1989 he became the chief red winemaker for the McWilliam's group, and his wines won major awards at Australian wine shows before he debuted his craft on BC soil.

"Like most Aussies, we needed to explore the world off the big island," explains Niva. "Before we had children, we did a lot of travelling through Europe and the US. We decided to move to Kelowna after a trip to Canada in the late '80s. When we realized there was actually a budding wine industry here, we thought it was a great opportunity to work and travel in a beautiful part of the world." They packed up with their two young daughters and started a new life here, with Jeff becoming the winemaker at Quails' Gate Winery. In 1999 they decided to take the plunge and purchase their own vineyard, naming it after Jeff's grandfather.

La Frenz's wine portfolio has won an impressive list of international awards. Their range of wines includes fortified wines and a notable port. Jeff's Chardonnay was one of the wines to draw the varietal back into the limelight, and he was one of the first to successfully make Viognier, a previously unknown variety in the BC wine industry. Jeff and Niva's daughters, Elise and Jessica, have both had incredible palates from a young age. Elise has followed her dad's footsteps into the wine world and is now managing the vineyards at La Frenz. Maybe wee granddaughter Aster will enter the family trade one day as well!

Chicken Cacciatore with Semolina Polenta

Niva Martin's parents come from a little place in Italy called Cavaso del Tomba, between Venice and Verona. This beautiful area boasts excellent risotto, polenta and tiramisu and is the birthplace of prosecco and grappa! Niva's mother taught her to cook many delicious dishes, including this rustic hunter's stew (*cacciatore* means "hunter" in Italian). Her mother made polenta with semolina (made from durum wheat) instead of cornmeal—it makes an amazing base for many stews and sauces.

Serves 4

Chicken Cacciatore:

8 bone-in, skin-on chicken thighs (about 3 lb)

¼ cup flour

3 Tbsp olive oil

1 large yellow onion, sliced into half rings

2 stalks celery, finely diced

2 cloves garlic, minced

4 cups sliced brown mushrooms

1 (796 ml/28 oz) can diced tomatoes, including the juice

1 cube chicken bouillon, crumbled

1 tsp salt

½ tsp pepper

Fresh sage leaves, to garnish (optional)

Semolina Polenta:

1 cup semolina

2 Tbsp butter

1 tsp salt

For the Chicken Cacciatore:

Dust the chicken thighs with the flour. In a saucepan over medium-high heat, heat 2 Tbsp of the olive oil and cook the chicken until browned, about 3 minutes per side. Remove and set aside.

Drain off any fat from the pan. Add the remaining 1 Tbsp olive oil to the pan, along with the onions, celery and garlic. Cook until the onions are soft, about 5 minutes. Add the sliced mushrooms and cook for 10 minutes, stirring often.

Return the chicken thighs to the pan, add the diced tomatoes and bring to a boil. Add the chicken bouillon, salt and pepper. Lower the heat to a simmer, cover and cook over low heat, stirring occasionally, until the chicken is cooked (about 1 hour).

For the Semolina Polenta:

Thirty minutes before the chicken is done, prepare the polenta.

In a medium-size pot, bring 4 cups salted water to a boil, then lower the heat to a slow boil. Gradually add the semolina, whisking to prevent lumps. Once all the semolina has been added and the mixture starts to thicken, turn the heat to low so it is just simmering, then cover and cook until thick and tender (about 20 minutes), stirring every 5 minutes or so to avoid burning. Add the butter, adjust the salt to taste and let sit for a few minutes.

Dollop a pile of polenta onto each plate and top with cacciatore, and a few fresh sage leaves, if you like. Mangia!

Pair with: La Frenz Reserve Pinot Noir. This elegant, delicate wine expresses layers of flavours as it opens in the glass, with raspberry bush and strawberry jam notes.

Ruby Blues Winery

www.rubyblueswinery.ca

917 Naramata Road, Penticton

R uby Blues is easy to spot on the Naramata Bench—look for the 1960s hippie van parked at the entrance of the winery, welcoming you with peace, love and good vibrations. There is plenty to see, from fabulous sculptures, paintings, mirrors and views to the colourful, welcoming wine shop. Inside, there is (of course) wine, but also many other delights, including Prudence Mahrer's exclusive line of shoes.

From the bodybuilding and fitness industry in Switzerland to farming (and becoming pilots!) in Naramata, Prudence and her husband Beat followed their hearts and built a dream. They created Ruby Blues Winery and its predecessor, Red Rooster Winery.

In 1997 they opened the original location for Red Rooster Winery (now Therapy Vineyards). In 2002 they made the shift to a larger property closer to the Penticton side of Naramata. They reopened Red Rooster Winery in record time, one year later in 2003. "Over the years, we planted 50 acres of vineyard on the Naramata Bench," says Prudence. "And when I say 'we,' I mean Beat and me. At that time there were no vineyard management companies to hire."

In 2003 life was crazy busy, and Peller Estates approached them to buy. They sold, but kept the property next door and continued to grow and sell grapes. Their shared spirit of adventure manifested in a new and different way: Beat and Prudence became commercial pilots and considered a flying business. But Prudence missed the customers. Beat did not miss the hustle and bustle of the wine shop, so the two made a deal: She would operate Ruby Blues Winery and deal with the public and sales, and they would not produce more than 7,000 or 8,000 cases. He would just have to look after the vineyards.

It worked. Together, Prudence and Beat (and winery dog Yoni) have won numerous awards, including an international award for their sparkling wine. Their signature line embodies their wonderful free spirits: peace and love and forever young.

Charlie's Äelplermagronen

Alpine Mac & Cheese

Who knew the Swiss had mac 'n' cheese nailed ages ago? Imagine mac 'n' cheese, but with good Gruyère, bacon and potatoes. Charlie Utz, Ruby Blues' general manager, has been with the winery since it opened—and he's also from Switzerland. According to him, this perfect winter meal is a very common dish in his homeland—an après-ski dream!

Serves 4

2 onions, thinly sliced

⅔ cup diced bacon

2 cloves garlic, minced

2 cups diced waxy potatoes (½-inch cubes)

2 cups vegetable stock

1 cup light cream

1 cup ziti or penne pasta

1 cup grated Gruyère cheese

Salt and pepper

3 Tbsp finely chopped curly parsley, to serve

Applesauce, to serve (optional)

In a large frying pan over medium heat, sauté the onions, bacon and garlic until the onions are caramelized and the bacon is crunchy, about 25–30 minutes. Remove the mixture to a dish and set aside.

Add the potatoes, stock and cream to the pan. Increase the heat to medium-high and bring to a light boil. Add the pasta, cover the pan with a lid and cook until the liquid is soaked into the pasta and the pasta is al dente, about 10–12 minutes. Remove from heat and stir in ½ cup of the Gruyère and the bacon and onion mixture. Add salt and pepper to taste. Divide between plates, top with parsley and serve with applesauce, if you like, and the remaining Gruyère on the side.

Pair with: Ruby Blues Red Stiletto. Stiletto is Ruby Blues' signature red blend, with a base of Syrah and some Merlot, Cabernet Sauvignon and Pinot varieties. Very light in tannin and fruity, with a smoky nose, this easy-sipping red wine pairs well with cedar-planked salmon on the barbecue or lamb chops.

D'Angelo Estate Winery

www.dangelowinery.com
979 Lochore Road, Penticton

All hail the Grape King! Sal D'Angelo is a familiar name in the Canadian wine industry—not only because he had vineyards and wineries operating in eastern and western Canada simultaneously, but also because in 1999 he was crowned Grape King in Niagara, an honour bestowed on grapegrowers for excellence in viticulture.

Although he was originally based in Niagara with a successful vineyard and winery operation, Sal began an annual research trip to the Okanagan in the late 1970s. Over time, his love for the west consumed him, and it became clear that the Naramata Bench would become his home and home to D'Angelo Estate Winery. He eventually purchased a stunning property in 2001 on Lochore Road, just west of Naramata Road, the main artery into wine country. The property slopes gently to the shores of Okanagan Lake, providing the optimal terroir to create his vision. For many years, Sal commuted from east to west to tend both vineyards, but in 2017 he sold in the east and formally became a westerner.

This is an old-school family winery: Two of Sal's three children work with him, Chris as assistant winemaker and Stephanie as operations manager. His brother Danny is on-site too, making the family's authentic panini recipes from his food truck. The tasting room sits just behind the family home and looks out toward the vineyards and the lake. They also have a B&B perfectly placed among the vines, complete with the same winery view. Amenities include an in-ground pool perfect for cooling off after a day of wine tasting.

Sal was born in Abruzzo but moved to eastern Canada with his family and a migration of other families from that region of Italy in the 1950s. Wine is an integral part of Italian culture, and Sal grew up with annual winemaking at home.

He is a hands-on winery owner and winemaker and can often be found doing the wine tastings himself in the wine shop. You want to talk about wine? This guy will give you his all. His passion for the craft and the land is still there after all these years in the industry, and his wine speaks to that. Sal is also known as a bit of a maverick in the winemaking world and is not afraid of experimentation. He has plans to plant red Montepulciano and white Trebbiano grapes, two varietals that are popular in his homeland, Abruzzo. There are also plans in the works to build a new three-storey winery—with two of those storeys underground!

Currently, D'Angelo Estate Winery is producing Merlot-Cabernet Franc, Merlot Malbec, Viognier, Pinot Noir, Miscela Tempranillo, Sette Coppa Riserva and a rosé. They are also known for their delicious port-style dessert wines Dolce Vita Rosso and Dolce Vita Bianca.

Sal is a man living his very best life.

Nonna's Panino

Sal D'Angelo's mother, Rosalina, made these delicious Italian sandwiches for her four hungry boys when they were growing up. His brother Danny has continued the tradition by opening a food truck at D'Angelo Estate Winery called Danelo's, which is open during the summer months. Panini make the perfect pairing for visiting wine tasters to enjoy with a glass of D'Angelo wine.

Serves 1

2 Tbsp pesto
1 focaccia bun, sliced in half
5 slices Genoa salami
2 slices Provolone cheese
1 sun-dried tomato or roasted red pepper, thinly sliced
2–3 thin slices marinated eggplant (available in jars at most Italian delis)
Olive oil, for drizzling

Spread 1 Tbsp of the pesto on each side of the bun, then layer the other ingredients on top and drizzle with olive oil.

If you have a panini press, set the temperature to medium and place the sandwich inside. Lightly press for 3 minutes to achieve a "half-pressed" sandwich. Cool slightly and serve.

If you do not have a press, preheat your oven to 350°F and warm the panino on a baking sheet for 5 minutes.

Pair with: D'Angelo Miscela Tempranillo. It begins with spicy blackberry and vanilla aromas, with boysenberry and dark chocolate on the palate and a lingering finish of vanilla. The texture is generous.

Bella Wines

www.bellawines.ca
4320 Gulch Road, Naramata

Jay Drysdale and Wendy Rose are Naramata homesteaders. On their beautiful farm and vineyard they are growing, raising and preserving food and making wine (one of life's most essential essentials). Jay grew up in Langley and Wendy hails from California. The two found each other in wine country and hung out their winery shingle in 2015. No ordinary winery, mind you—Bella Wines is the Okanagan's only boutique sparkling wine house, and they have been a dazzling triumph.

Jay was formerly a chef, and for him, being able to farm and create wine is the ultimate dream. He found the ideal mate in Wendy—with a mother who was friends with Alice Waters, this is a lifestyle that Wendy was made for. Their winery and tasting room are located deep in Naramata, almost at the end of the winery-laden thoroughfare. A winding road will take you down through the vineyard and back up to their little slice of heaven. Warning: You might be feverishly greeted by an adorable bulldog named Buddha, who may or may not have a posse of pigs behind her . . . and who may or may not race you to the tasting room.

Time to get your bubble on! What is ultra-special about this sparkling wine house is that they have created a range of single-varietal sparkling wines. A tasting here offers a full lesson and exercise in terroir: You can taste the exact same varietal from totally different regions (they source from six different areas) and experience firsthand the huge difference that "place" makes. And then you will become a wine geek.

Most of the wines are made in the traditional method: bottle-fermented, hand-riddled and hand-disgorged. And then there is the méthode ancestrale. Bella is the maker of the very first natural ancestrale sparkling wine in western Canada. It is basically making sparkling wine the old-school way, like the monks did back in the 15th century. It is kind of a miracle, and the process is totally hands-off. There is absolutely no flirting with this grape juice—it is whole-cluster pressed, then the juice wild-ferments in a neutral barrel, and at the perfect moment, it is hand-bottled. This is Mother Nature–style wine (well, with a little help from Jay).

There is no eatery here yet, but we can hope and dream. Jay and Wendy do have a hand in the culinary scene and are heavily into their community, hosting al fresco dinners and other special events on the farm. For now, enjoy the other eateries in the area—like Legend Distilling up the way, which offers a fabulous array of local libations to tempt your palate and a seasonal patio restaurant.

Bella Stinging Nettle Pasta with Carbonara Sauce

"One of the reasons we love this dish so much is because it uses staples of our farm pantry," says Bella Wines' Jay Drysdale. "If you cure your own meats from the animals you have raised, this simple dish takes on a different decadence. And when the eggs are from your own chickens, you trust the quality and truly respect the ingredient. If you aren't making the pasta from scratch, this whole dish can be completed in about 15 minutes."

Serves 4

8 strips bacon, cut into small strips or cubes

2 eggs, beaten

¼ cup grated Parmesan cheese, plus more to garnish

1½ Tbsp pepper, or to taste

1 lb fresh tagliatelle (see note) or store-bought

Chopped chives, to garnish

Note: Stinging nettle is a wild, edible plant that grows locally and has many medicinal superpowers. It is kind of fussy to harvest (hence the "stinging" part), but worth it. Wendy and Jay like to make their own stinging nettle pasta. They forage and pick stinging nettle, bundle and hang it to dry, then pulverize it into a powder and mix 3 Tbsp of the powder into their pasta dough. If you don't have access to stinging nettle, try blending a mix of your favourite herbs into your pasta dough, or simply opt for store-bought.

In a frying pan over medium heat, fully cook the bacon. Drain on paper towel.

In a large bowl, mix the eggs and stir in the Parmesan cheese and pepper.

Fill a large pot with water, bring to a boil and add the pasta. Cook the pasta for 4–7 minutes or until al dente.

When the pasta is ready, quickly drain it and immediately add to the bowl of beaten eggs. Let the pasta sit in the egg mixture for 1 minute, then toss and season. The hot pasta will cook the eggs into a creamy sauce. Add the cooked bacon and mix in. Garnish with chives and grated Parmesan.

Buon appetito!

Pair with: Bella Wines Methode Ancestrale Rosé. This special bubbly is a Gamay Noir "pét-nat" from Mariani Vineyard in Naramata. (In the US, méthode ancestrale is commonly referred to as "pét-nat," short for pétillant naturel.) This unique wine has an orange hue, and it opens up with an intense expression of peach and grapefruit.

Meyer Family Vineyards

www.mfvwines.com
4287 McLean Creek Road, Okanagan Falls

Just outside of the tiny town of Okanagan Falls, under the iridescent face of Peach Cliff, lies Meyer Family Vineyards. Specializing in Pinot Noir and Chardonnay, this celebrated winery was one of the first to cross the pond with sales in the UK and other destinations abroad. JAK Meyer and Janice Stevens didn't plan on becoming vintners. But as seems to be the case for many in the wine business, an irresistible vineyard opportunity presented itself and the couple jumped in.

Their first vineyard purchase was a lakeview property on Naramata Bench, and they found their second property on McLean Creek Road in Okanagan Falls. This rolling property became their family home, with daughters Camryn and Sydney and winery dog Bruce all on board for the vineyard life. Having two vineyards allowed them to create a range of Chardonnay and Pinot Noir labels, all bringing the unique characteristics of the differentiating terroir. Winemaker Chris Carson is the man behind the wines.

JAK and Janice have become known for their hospitality and their fabulous wine club parties. The lovely wine shop and winery are in the valley below their house. The "wine lounge" outside the tasting room is a great spot to hang out and have a glass of wine or a bite to eat from the fun "build your own charcuterie" menu featuring plenty of delicious local food items. You can also opt for a private, guided sit-down tasting of their single-vineyard premium wines in a beautiful outdoor cabana area.

JAK and Janice love being a part of the Okanagan Falls wine community. "It's a small jewel of an area with great soils, slopes and a sense of community," says JAK. "We have one of the best and most admired winery associations in the Okanagan, with everyone working together and being friends."

The Meyer brand continues to win awards, build on its huge fan base and achieve high praise from critics. JAK also played an integral role in the creation of the BC Pinot Noir Celebration, a festival featuring BC's most stellar wines from this varietal—one of his proudest achievements.

Janice's Chicken Marbella

Based on the classic dish from *The Silver Palate Cookbook*, this fail-safe crowd-pleaser has become Janice Stevens-Meyer's signature dinner party dish and a family favourite. This is one of those stress-free make-ahead meals—just marinate all the ingredients together the night before and put the entire thing into the oven to roast the next day. Gather around the table with friends or family and serve it with brown rice or pearl couscous, a simple green salad and crusty bread. Cheers!

Serves 6–8

1 cup dry white wine

½ cup chopped dried figs

½ cup chopped dried apricots

½ cup pitted dried prunes

¼ cup pitted green olives (see note)

¼ cup capers + a splash of juice from the jar

¼ cup red wine vinegar

¼ cup olive oil

6 cloves garlic, halved if large

1 Tbsp dried oregano

2 tsp salt

2 tsp pepper

5 lb free-range, organic chicken thighs (see note)

2 Tbsp chopped flat-leaf parsley, to serve

Notes: If you don't have chicken thighs on hand, feel free to substitute a different cut. For the olives, Janice prefers to use Spanish, but any will work.

In a large glass bowl with a lid (or a ziplock bag), combine all the ingredients, except the chicken and parsley. Add the chicken and submerge in the marinade to cover completely. Marinate overnight in the fridge, turning the chicken a couple of times to make sure the flavours are evenly distributed.

The next day, preheat the oven to 350°F. Arrange the chicken on a large baking pan and pour the marinade overtop. Cook, basting frequently, until the juices run clear when a sharp knife is inserted into the thickest point of the thigh, about 50–60 minutes.

Serve family-style in a large shallow bowl and sprinkle with parsley to garnish.

Pair with: Meyer Family Vineyards Old Block Pinot Noir. The Pinot Noir Old Block is one of the original vineyard plantings from 1994. It has a beautiful elegance, with dark cherry and savoury notes. The palate is well structured with hints of forest berries, baked rhubarb and spice.

Wild Goose Vineyards

www.wildgoosewinery.com
2145 Sun Valley Way, Okanagan Falls

Located in picturesque Okanagan Falls, surrounded by rolling vineyards, the welcoming tasting room at Wild Goose Vineyards has the special feel only found at a quintessential family-run winery. That ambiance spills over into the casual bistro overlooking the vines, where you can enjoy delicious German-style food, including the wood-fire–smoked ribs that the family enjoys so much.

Adolf "Fritz" Kruger immigrated to Winnipeg from Germany in 1951. At age 52 and semi-retired, he ventured to the Okanagan to visit a friend with a vineyard. Captivated by the land, he convinced his sons, Roland and Hagen, to purchase the 10-acre parcel of farmland in Okanagan Falls that would become Wild Goose in 1984. The two have continued their father's dream and built a legendary brand in the Canadian wine industry.

The 1980s were a tempestuous time in the burgeoning Okanagan wine industry, and the rules and regulations were not keeping up with the industry's growth. Adolf was a passionate lobbyist working to change the licensing regulations that restricted wine sales direct from the winery. His determination paid off, and in 1990 Wild Goose was issued a licence to become BC's first farmgate winery—allowing it to grow, produce and bottle the wines on-site. This marked a huge turning point for the industry and encouraged other wineries to build businesses as well. Adolf went on to help set up the BC Wine Institute, which initiated quality standards, approval and certification for wines made with 100% BC grapes.

Since then, Roland, Hagen and their families have built a highly recognized wine label and won an extraordinary number of awards. Their pride and passion for the craft is evident at the winery, as is the warmth of the family. "Being BC's first farmgate to grow, vint and bottle on-site was an exciting achievement back in 1990," says Roland, "and still being in business as the original owners today is something we are very proud of."

Hagen has passed the role of winemaker to his son Nicholas, who has inherited his father's gift. "Nik is driven by Hagen, who has produced some of the best and most consistent wines in British Columbia for over 20 years," says Roland. "With Hagen as his mentor, Nik has learned to start with the best fruit possible and to nurture it the entire way, from crush pad to bottle. Like his father and his opa before him, he is meticulous with his winemaking practice and never takes shortcuts."

From its start as a farmgate winery producing 500 cases in 1990, Wild Goose has grown to a production capacity nearing 25,000 cases today.

Oma's Rouladen

Hagen and Roland Kruger's mother was a wonderful cook who left many family recipes. Roland jokes that they never had measurements, but this is what they have come up with over the years. Rouladen—a wonderful German comfort food—is basically beef rolled with mustard, pickles and bacon. When it's served over spaetzle with a warm potato salad made with bacon drippings (see page 123), how could you go wrong?

Serves 6

6 thin slices steak (see note)
Salt and pepper
4 Tbsp grainy or yellow mustard
8 oz bacon, cubed
1½ large onions, diced
6 small dill pickles
2 Tbsp grapeseed oil or olive oil
3 cups beef stock (see note)
2½ Tbsp cornstarch
Spaetzle, to serve
Sliced cucumber, to serve (optional)

Notes: For the steak, ask your butcher to cut pieces for rouladen—4 × 6-inch pieces are perfect. If you like, substitute red wine for some of the beef stock.

Preheat the oven to 350°F.

Season the steak slices with salt and pepper, then lay them out and cover each slice with a thin layer of mustard. Sprinkle with all of the bacon and half of the onions. Place a small dill pickle at one end of a slice of meat, then roll the meat around it into a bundle, tucking in the ends. Secure the roll with a skewer or toothpick, and repeat with the remaining slices.

In a Dutch oven or a heavy cast-iron pot with a lid over medium-high heat, heat the oil. Add the rouladen and cook until brown on all sides, about 5 minutes. Remove from the pot and set aside.

Add the remaining onions to the pot and sauté until lightly browned, about 5–7 minutes, then add the beef stock and continue to cook over medium heat for 2–3 minutes.

In a small bowl, stir the cornstarch with ½ cup cold water until it is fully dissolved. Slowly add the mixture to the broth, stirring until thickened. Return the rouladen to the pot, cover and bake in the oven until tender, about 1 hour.

Serve one rouladen per person over spaetzle, with a side of potato salad (see page 123). If you like, plate with sliced cucumbers.

Pair with: Wild Goose Vineyards Red Horizon Meritage. This classic Bordeaux-style blend of estate grapes has an intense dark colour, well-integrated silky tannins and a luscious mouthfeel. Aromas of pepper, dried fig, cherry, dark fruit and cassis are followed by hints of licorice, leather, chocolate and smoke.

German Potato Salad

Unlike many traditional types, real German potato salad doesn't use mayonnaise. These potatoes are tarted up with vinegar instead, which gives the salad a real zing and helps balance the bacon drippings. This is as good as it sounds!

Serves 6

2 lb small new potatoes

2 Tbsp grapeseed oil or olive oil + more to moisten

1 large onion, diced

8 oz bacon, diced

2 Tbsp white vinegar, or to taste

Salt and pepper

2 hard-boiled eggs, diced

4 medium dill pickles, diced

In a large pot of water, boil the potatoes until tender, then peel while still warm and thickly slice. Set aside.

In a frying pan over medium-high heat, heat the oil. Add the onions and bacon and fry together until the onions are softened and the bacon is browned. Let the mixture cool slightly, then transfer to a large bowl, including all the drippings from the frying pan (this is the secret to this entire recipe!).

Add vinegar, salt and pepper to taste to the bowl. Depending on the amount of bacon drippings, you may need to moisten with a little more oil.

Add the eggs and dill pickles and gently mix all the ingredients together by hand, being careful not to overmix and break the potatoes. The salad should have a slightly moist consistency and a slightly vinegary zing.

Serve just warm or at room temperature. Any remaining salad can be stored in the fridge for a couple of days.

Pair with: Wild Goose Autumn Gold. Equal parts Riesling, Gewürztraminer and Pinot Blanc, this clean, crisp white wine carries aromas of orchard fruit, apricot and anise.

Nighthawk Vineyards

www.nighthawkvineyards.com
2735 Green Lake Road, Okanagan Falls

As you turn off the highway into Okanagan Falls, you will begin to climb a hill on a rugged rural road. Just when you think that you must have taken a wrong turn, you will round the corner and feast your eyes on a massive hillside of rolling vineyards. Travel a little farther and you will melt at the sight of tranquil Green Lake ahead, where a vineyard and a huge log-style home sit on the far side like a dream. This is Nighthawk Vineyards, a boutique, family-run farmgate winery experience.

The Bibby family—Daniel and Christy and their four children—are all involved in the food and wine industry. Daniel was first an executive chef and then eventually became general manager of several hotels and resorts. He and Christy met in Kelowna in 1993, when Daniel was a sous chef at the Grand Okanagan and Christy worked at the Hotel Eldorado.

Their dream evolved organically. "We were always very connected to the food and wine industry and have been excited to see the evolution of Okanagan wines," Christy says. "In 2008 we spent a weekend in the spring down at Burrowing Owl, and as we had coffee overlooking the vineyards . . . that sealed the deal. As we drove back to Kelowna, we started looking for small vineyards for sale. We found the property of our dreams overlooking Green Lake in Okanagan Falls, but it would take us another four years to complete the purchase. During that time, our family took a few vineyard courses and volunteered at wineries owned by friends of ours to make sure we enjoyed the farming side, as that is where the wine comes to life."

There is some farming to be found in their DNA. Fun fact: Christy's great-uncle from generations back (born 1742 in Loch Lomond, Scotland) moved to the American colony in 1770, settled in Fredericksburg and was hired by George Washington as his gardener—including the farming of grapes!

The Bibby kids all grew up working in the food and wine industry and have carved out their own passionate careers from it. Dylan is a level 3 sommelier and has worked for several wineries in the area; Meagan is a baker, and she and her husband Ian own the Lake Village Bakery in Osoyoos; Dakota took both the viticulture and winery assistant programs at Okanagan College and is now the winemaker at Nighthawk Vineyards; and Carson studied through the culinary arts program at Okanagan College and has just returned from Ottawa, where he worked under Chef Marc Lepine at Atelier. Basically, the Bibbys are experts on all things food and wine.

Nighthawk's small but mighty team is working on expanding their current wine production and has plans to add a scenic outdoor patio and kitchen overlooking the vineyard. Another long-term goal is to build exclusive accommodations that will connect guests with the land, including a farm-/vine-to-table culinary experience on the vineyard.

Nighthawk Vineyards Cassoulet

Cassoulet is a traditional peasant-style bean stew that originated in southern France. The Bibby family typically uses their slow cooker to braise the cassoulet while they are all out working in the vineyards during harvest, so when the team comes in for lunch, the house is filled with the wonderful aroma of hearty comfort food. The dish is simple, yet incredibly flavourful, and helps provide the energy required to keep picking.

Serves 6–8

2 cups dry white beans
2 Tbsp duck fat or peanut oil
4 bone-in, skin-on chicken thighs
Sea salt and pepper
4 oz pork belly, diced
2 medium onions, finely diced
1 carrot, finely diced
1 stalk celery, finely diced
2 cloves garlic, minced
½ cup white wine (like Nighthawk Chardonnay)
4 oz chorizo sausage, diced
2 cups chicken stock
1 tsp chopped lemon thyme or regular thyme leaves
1 sprig rosemary
1 bay leaf

Note: *This cassoulet can also be made as a vegetarian dish. Swap the chicken for 2 roasted poblano chili peppers, leave out the pork belly and chorizo, use vegetable stock instead of chicken stock and add 2 Tbsp julienned sun-dried tomatoes along with the garlic.*

Cover the beans with water and soak overnight.

In a sauté pan over high heat, heat the duck fat and sear both sides of the chicken thighs, about 2 minutes per side. Season with salt and pepper. Remove the chicken from the pan and put it in a large slow cooker.

Using the same pan, sauté the pork belly until golden brown. Add the onions, carrots and celery, cook for 5 minutes, then add the garlic. Cook for another minute, then deglaze the pan with the white wine and transfer the contents to the slow cooker.

Drain the beans and add to the slow cooker along with the chorizo, chicken stock, thyme, rosemary and bay leaf. Cook on the high setting for 6 hours, or until the beans are tender.

Remove the chicken from the bones, shred the meat and add it back into the cassoulet.

Season with salt and pepper to taste.

Pair with: Nighthawk Vineyards Chardonnay. Aged for eight months in French oak, this delicate wine features aromatic elegance and mineral complexity distinctive to this high-altitude vineyard. It is silky and smooth on the mid-palate, with a crisp, long finish.

Burrowing Owl Estate Winery (page 165)

Oliver,
Osoyoos &
Similkameen
Valley

Oliver

Osoyoos

Similkameen Valley

Introduction

The landscape dramatically changes as you head south through the Okanagan into desert country. This region is located at the tip of the Sonoran Desert, which runs up from Mexico through California and parts of Arizona and is Canada's only arid desert. The desert hills of Oliver lay claim to some of the most famous winelands in BC, and the landscape and conditions have been compared to Tuscany's.

Between Oliver and Osoyoos, the vineyard-lined Black Sage Bench and illustrious Golden Mile Bench face each other across a valley. The hot, dry climate makes this region ideal to grow grapes and create the big, beautiful red wines that it is celebrated for. Continue south almost to the US border to find Osoyoos. Small yet well known to vacationers, it offers hot summers, lake activities and, more recently, salmon fishing! After the Okanagan Nation Alliance spent years rebuilding the region's natural waterways, sockeye salmon have returned to their native waters to spawn (read more about this on page 171).

A side trip west into the Similkameen Valley is a magical experience with a dramatic entrance. As you round the bend on the hillside above, you will see a lush green valley below lying in the protective arms of a craggy, rugged mountain range. This valley offers farms and vineyards the ideal conditions for agriculture and growing superb grapes. And the community focuses on organic growing and sustainable farming to protect the future of its special land and waters, which produce such outstanding wines and fruit.

Covert Farms Family Estate

www.covertfarms.ca
300 Covert Place, Oliver

Covert Farms grows good food, good wine and good people. Now in their third generation of farmers, the Covert family operates a 650-acre organic farm on a stunning piece of desert land in Oliver that is also home to a rare antelope-brush ecosystem.

This is no ordinary winery tour visit—it is a full-on farm experience. Visitors to the farm have plenty of options: shop for produce or pick your own vegetables from the u-pick gardens, taste wines, feed the longhorn cows, marvel at the staggering backdrop of McIntyre Bluff (a famous Okanagan landmark), go for a hike or hop on the back of an old pickup truck for a tour of it all.

The Covert name epitomizes community, leadership and a trusted stewardship of BC farmland. Each generation of the family has offered progressive solutions to farming and found new ways to grow the healthiest crops for people and our planet.

In 1959, while running a tomato-shipping business in California, George Covert became fascinated with news of farming opportunities in the Okanagan. He made the trip and purchased a large undeveloped plateau of land north of Oliver on a whim, and moved there with his wife Winifred. In the early 1960s, his first crops were born, with 100 successful acres each of onions and tomatoes—and he planted a vineyard.

George passed away in 1996, leaving the business in the hands of his son Mike. Together with his wife Diana and their son Gene, Mike continued to build on George's legacy and made a series of contributions to the agriculture industry of the Okanagan.

After Mike passed away at the young age of 60 in 2004, Gene carried on with the help of his wife Shelly, mom Diana, grandma Winifred and aunt Ashley—a female-supported tour de force! They decided to go organic, and by 2006 they had a certified organic market garden and had managed to get their entire 142 acres certified. That included grapes, vegetables and fruit. Gene and Shelly's four kids have been very involved on the farm and were raised the old-fashioned way: with hard work and a lot of love. The winery opened in 2005, with Gene eventually taking the reins as winemaker, and produces a range of award-winning wines from their estate-grown, certified organic, biodynamic vineyards.

Diana's Fried Green Tomatoes

When you're part of a sustainable farming family, you learn how to make the best use of your crops and to preserve them. Green, unripened tomatoes are usually plentiful at the end of the season, but many people lack ideas on how to use them. Made famous by the 1991 movie *Fried Green Tomatoes*, this delightful dish is a great way to celebrate the end of harvest. These store beautifully in the fridge and reheat well, so make a pile while you're at it.

Serves 4–6

3 large green tomatoes (preferably with a touch of orange blush)
1 cup flour
Seasoning salt, to taste
2 eggs
2 cups breadcrumbs (see note)
½ tsp chopped thyme leaves
Pepper
½ cup butter

Note: Diana makes this recipe with Viennese-style breadcrumbs, but you can make them with your favourite crumbs. Crushed saltines are also amazing!

Set out a sheet of waxed or parchment paper for the prepared tomatoes.

Cut the tops and bottoms off the tomatoes and cut the remainder into ¼- to ½-inch-thick slices. Set aside.

Line up three bowls as a dipping station for the tomatoes. In the first bowl, mix the flour with a sprinkle of seasoning salt. In the second bowl, beat the eggs. In the third bowl, mix the breadcrumbs with the thyme, pepper and another sprinkle of seasoning salt.

Heat a frying pan on medium-low or a thermostatic griddle on medium-low or 250°F–275°F.

Dredge each slice of tomato in the flour, then coat with the egg, letting the excess drip off, then submerge in crumbs to coat. Place the coated tomatoes on parchment paper until you are ready to fry.

Melt the butter in the pan or on the griddle, then add the tomato slices. Cook for about 5 minutes per side or until golden brown and tender inside.

Serve hot for breakfast or as a starter or a side dish with barbecued steak.

Pair with: Covert Farms Family Estate Roussanne Viognier. Opulent and juicy, with flavours of dried apricots, preserved lemons and white peach, this wine will seduce you with a generous yet complicated finish.

Chiles Rellenos

Why a Mexican dish? George and Winifred Covert used to have a farming venture in Guaymas, Sonora, California and the cook there taught Winifred how to make Mexican food. Chiles rellenos (poblano chili peppers stuffed with cheese and deep-fried) was one of their favourites, so Diana Covert made it her special mission to learn how to make this dish for her in-laws. The tradition has continued, and Diana has been serving them at special occasions like birthdays and Thanksgiving for over 40 years. Add sides of rice and salad to turn this into a main course.

If you want to prepare this dish ahead, leave the chilies to cool after frying and then wrap and refrigerate or freeze. The sauce can also be refrigerated or frozen to use later, so this entire dish can be served anytime.

Serves 4 as an appetizer

Tomato Sauce:

1 medium sweet onion, chopped

1 clove garlic, minced

2 Tbsp olive oil

3 cups chicken stock

1 (796 ml/28 oz) can crushed Roma tomatoes or 4–5 very ripe Roma tomatoes, chopped

1 tsp dried oregano

1 tsp ground cumin

1 tsp chili powder, or to taste

½ tsp salt

Chiles Rellenos:

1 cup grated Monterey Jack cheese

⅓ cup grated Fontina cheese

1 tsp dried marjoram

4 poblano chili peppers

2 large eggs, separated

2 Tbsp flour + more for coating chilies (see note)

Peanut oil, for frying (see note)

Sliced green onions, to serve (optional)

Sour cream, to serve (optional)

For the Tomato Sauce:

In a large saucepan over medium heat, sauté the onions and garlic in the olive oil until translucent, then add the chicken stock, crushed tomatoes and seasonings. Simmer for 25–30 minutes, then taste and adjust the seasoning if necessary. Set aside for serving.

For the Chiles Rellenos:

In a bowl, mix the cheeses together. Rub the marjoram between your hands over the mixture and add it to the bowl. Using your hands, squeeze the cheese into football-shaped balls that will fit into the chilies.

Roast the chilies directly over the flame on a gas-stove grill, on a barbecue or in the oven at 500°F, turning to blacken evenly. When the skin has blackened, drop the chilies into a paper bag and close the top for about 10 minutes to steam and loosen the skin from the flesh. Rub the burnt skin off under running water, being careful not to tear the flesh.

Carefully make a 2-inch incision in the side of each chili to extract the seeds with a small spoon (this is where the heat is). You want to keep the chili as intact as possible so that the cheese-ball stuffing will stay in while it's cooking. Insert a ball of cheese into each chili through that same incision and lay the stuffed chilies on waxed paper or a plate.

To make the batter, beat the egg whites until they form soft peaks. Add the flour and gently blend. In a separate bowl, beat the egg yolks, then gently fold them into the egg white/flour mixture to achieve a light, fluffy batter.

continued

Notes: For a gluten-free version of this recipe, try Bob's Red Mill Gluten Free All-Purpose Baking Flour in the egg batter. Use rice flour to coat the chilies before frying, as it adheres better. Chiles rellenos are traditionally fried in lard. Diana uses peanut oil, but feel free to use any oil of your preference.

Preheat the oven to 300°F and heat the oil in a Dutch oven or large, heavy frying pan until almost smoking. Lightly flour the stuffed chilies and use a large spoon to dip them into the batter one at a time, rolling to coat all sides, before adding to the hot oil to deep-fry. Sometimes the cheese will bubble out while you're cooking, especially if the chili defied all your efforts to cut a neat hole in the side. It's messy, but it won't all drain out. To prevent the chilies from cooking only on one side, Diana's trick is to immediately ladle some oil over the raw batter side. Then continue to cook the chilies, turning, until they turn golden. Remove from the pan and drain on paper towels.

Arrange the fried chilies in a casserole dish or your favourite Mexican serving dish. Pour the tomato sauce overtop and cover with aluminum foil. Bake for 35–45 minutes, or until heated through.

To serve, carefully place a chile relleno with sauce on each plate. If you like, garnish with green onions and sour cream.

Pair with: Covert Farms Family Estate Grand Reserve Pinot Noir. Aged in French oak for 21 months, this wine has a juicy bouquet of cherry blossoms, plums and cinnamon framed with notes of Japanese maple and milk chocolate.

The BC Wine Lover's Cookbook

Quinta Ferreira Estate Winery

www.quintaferreira.com
6094 Black Sage Road, Oliver

In Portuguese, *quinta* means two things. First, it means "five," which represents John and Maria Ferreira and their three children. It also means "estate," and is the way wineries are traditionally named in Portugal (Quinta + last name of family owners). Quinta Ferreira Estate Winery is a celebration of family and of love—for one another, for tradition and for the art of winemaking.

The architecture of the winery, or *adega* (wine house), is adobe-style, like the wineries of Portugal. The beautiful wine shop radiates the warmth and spirit of this kind and welcoming family and features original art from Maria's sister, Carmen Tome. There are flower gardens and a patio with tables to linger at and soak in the atmosphere, and you can sip wine and bring a picnic or purchase a selection of meats, cheeses, olives and crackers from the deli fridge.

Both born in Portugal, John and Maria immigrated to Canada as children with their families in the early 1960s and grew up in Oliver's community of immigrant farming families. Many Portuguese families were coming to the South Okanagan to farm during that time. The climate produced bountiful crops and offered a wonderful opportunity to begin a new life growing field crops and orcharding. After starting their own family, John and Maria spent some time helping on their family farms. Later on, they purchased John's parents' orchard, added a packinghouse operation on their land and became successful exporters of fruit across the country.

After 20 years in fruit, the Ferreiras decided to make the change to grapes. They began the transition in 1999, and over the years they planted Syrah, Malbec, Petite Verdot, Viognier, Sauvignon Blanc, Zinfandel, Touriga Nacional and Cabernet Sauvignon. Initially they were only growing the grapes to sell, but then their son Michael decided to become a winemaker. The family opened Quinta Ferreira Estate Winery in June 2007 and has since built a reputation for fine wines. The entire family continues to play a role in the business with pride.

Pai's Bifanas

Portuguese Pork in a Bun

Bifanas are a common and popular dish in Portugal. In the early 1980s, Maria Ferreira's pai (dad) used to make these for events at the local soccer and Portuguese clubs. "His secret was to marinate them in a lot of wine, spices and garlic. The aroma would draw people from all around," says Maria. Quinta Ferreira continues the family tradition during the Okanagan Spring Wine Festival with their annual Bifanas, Wine & Live Music event. To reduce prep time, you can serve this with sliced raw onions instead of caramelized.

Serves 6

1 lb pork loin

½ cup white wine

1 large bay leaf

1 tsp garlic powder or 1 clove garlic, minced

½ tsp seasoning salt

½ tsp paprika

½ tsp dried onions

Dash of Tabasco sauce

⅓ cup + 1 Tbsp vegetable oil

2 large onions, thickly sliced

6 Portuguese buns, to serve

6 lettuce leaves, to serve

6 slices tomato, to serve

Thinly slice the pork loin and place in a bowl. Cover with the wine, bay leaf, all of the spices and the Tabasco. Mix to ensure that the pork is fully covered, cover the bowl and marinate in the fridge overnight.

The next day, remove the bowl from the fridge. In a large frying pan over high heat, heat ⅓ cup of the vegetable oil, then add the marinated meat and the bay leaf, reserving the marinade. Quickly fry the pork for about 1–2 minutes on each side, then pour in the marinade, letting it bubble. Continue frying for another minute per side, then remove from the pan.

In another frying pan over medium-high heat, heat 1 Tbsp of the oil and sauté the onions until tender and slightly caramelized. Remove to a plate for serving.

To serve, slice the Portuguese buns in half and add a slice of pork, lettuce, tomato and sautéed onions. Maria recommends a side of coleslaw and fries.

Pair with: Quinta Ferreira Merlot. Richly coloured and bursting with intense aromas of vanilla, black cherry, cinnamon and cloves, this wine is complex and well balanced. Soft tannins frame flavours of black pepper, plums, blackberries and chocolate that linger through to the finish. It's delicious on its own or with grilled meats.

Le Vieux Pin Winery

www.levieuxpin.ca
5496 Black Sage Road, Oliver

Prepare to be utterly enchanted when you discover Le Vieux Pin Winery on Black Sage Road. The vineyards of this charming estate surround a petite Provençal-style winery build-ing, picture-perfect with its gravel courtyard, little wrought-iron tables and chairs and aromatic lavender bushes scenting the air. Inside, a chalkboard listing les vins de la maison is featured beside the cozy tasting bar. The pièce de résistance is Severine (Sev) Pinte, a French winemaker and viticulturist and the face and spirit behind the winery operation. She has combined her knowledge of old-world French winemaking with new-world Okanagan style, and the result has been phenomenal.

Le Vieux Pin literally translates to "the old pine tree" and is a tribute to the majestic old pine tree on the winery estate. Le Vieux Pin has excelled in creating stellar Syrah and has a cult following for the purpose-grown Vaila rosé. It is one of the most finely crafted rosés in the province, and one of the first to be made in the traditional French style. "For me, rosé is one of the most challenging styles of wine to create," Sev explains. Critics have called it "sunshine captured in a bottle."

With a degree in agronomy from the esteemed Montpellier University and a master's degree in viticulture and oenology, Sev is what the French call a vigneron. She spent many years honing her craft in France before coming here in 2010, and she uses sustainable and organic farming practices in the vineyards. She adheres to strong ethics and a philosophy that includes "keeping our farm healthy and devoid of chemicals for our children and our children's children."

Winery owners Saeedeh and Sean Salem emigrated from Iran and own two of Oliver's most stylish small wineries: Le Vieux Pin and LaStella Winery. They are passionate food and wine lovers and found the perfect match in Sev to make their dream winery a reality. "When I first arrived to become the winemaker at Le Vieux Pin, it felt like it was meant to be," Sev recalls.

The owners have an Italian-inspired villa for rent called the Lakehouse on Osoyoos Lake.

Pair with: Le Vieux Pin Ava. Named for winemaker Sev's daughter, Ava is an elegant blend of traditional white Rhône varietals: Viognier, Marsanne and Roussanne. Redhaven peaches and yellow plums mingle with white aromatic flowers, herbal tea and light brioche notes.

Mamie's Scallops à la Flamande

As a child, Le Vieux Pin's Severine Pinte spent idyllic summers at her grandparents' cottage in the French countryside, near the small fishing village of Étaples. "We used to drive to the dock early in the mornings," says Sev, "and I would watch, completely mesmerized, as the fishermen quickly opened and released the scallops from the shells. Once home, my mamie would patiently clean the scallops, remove the sand and prepare them to make this dish." For Sev, this recipe brings back sweet memories of her home in France.

Serves 6

Scallops:

18 medium scallops

2 Tbsp butter

4 cups small white mushrooms, halved or quartered depending on size

1 cup white wine (preferably Le Vieux Pin Petit Blanc)

Juice of 1 lemon

Béchamel Sauce:

2 Tbsp butter

4 shallots, very thinly sliced

2 Tbsp flour

1 cup white wine (preferably Le Vieux Pin Petit Blanc)

½ cup finely chopped flat-leaf parsley

Salt and pepper

Assembly:

½ cup fine breadcrumbs

½ cup grated Emmenthal cheese

Note: *Severine likes to serve this dish on scallop shells, which can be purchased at many kitchen stores. Alternatively, you can use small ramekins.*

For the Scallops:

Clean the scallops under cold water and pat dry with paper towel.

In a frying pan over low heat, melt the butter and sauté the scallops for about 5 minutes, or until slightly golden on both sides. Set aside.

In a medium saucepan over medium-high heat, bring the mushrooms, wine, lemon juice and ¼ cup of water to a simmer for 10 minutes.

Drain the mushrooms, reserving the liquid for the béchamel sauce.

For the Béchamel Sauce:

In a large saucepan over low heat, melt the butter and sauté the shallots until golden brown.

Stir in the flour until all of the butter has been absorbed, then slowly add the reserved liquid from the mushrooms, continuously stirring. Add the white wine. Continue stirring until the béchamel thickens and you can see one or two bubbles coming up, then remove from heat. Stir in the parsley and salt and pepper to taste.

To Assemble:

Preheat the oven to broil.

Place three scallops in each scallop shell (or small ramekin) and scatter the mushrooms evenly over each. Top with about 2 Tbsp béchamel sauce per shell and line them up on a parchment-lined baking sheet.

Sprinkle each serving with breadcrumbs and Emmenthal cheese and broil until the cheese is melted and golden, about 2–3 minutes.

Serve immediately.

vinAmité Cellars

www.vinamitecellars.com
5381 Highway 97, Oliver

Bienvenue to vinAmité Cellars! Wendy and Ray Coulombe and their two daughters, Nathalie and Catherine, have added real French flair to Oliver's famous Golden Mile, with their fabulous French Canadian style and their creative genius. The family includes artists, gourmands, designers and even a fashionista. On top of that, they are wonderfully welcoming, warm and charming.

vinAmité is a small garagiste-style operation (see page 274) with unstoppable joie de vivre. The walls in the cozy tasting room feature Nathalie's beautiful art, and the tasting bar is artfully stacked with wines co-created by winemakers Ray and Catherine. With a culinary background, Catherine has also ensured that the gastronomic offering is covered, with housemade charcuterie and cheese and a patio that provides the perfect view and ambiance to sit and savour it.

The child of immigrants from France, Ray grew up with a nurtured palate. "Dad's roots go back to Isle de France outside Paris," he shares, "while Mom's heritage comes from the farmlands of Carcassonne, farther south. They met in Alberta . . . their parents were original pioneer settlers of the newly formed province of Alberta." Ray graduated with a Bachelor of Fine Arts from the ArtCenter College of Design in Los Angeles and ended up in Montreal.

Wendy also has a European background, but her family (last name Chancey—there is a long and wonderful story regarding the origins of that name that you must ask her about) moved to Dearborn (near Detroit) from Europe during the Depression to work in the factories. Wendy pursued a career as a graphic artist, and fell in love with the city of Montreal while travelling there, where she later met Ray.

Once grown, both their daughters moved away to pursue their own passions. "As empty nesters, Wendy and I travelled until 2008, when we purchased the house on the hill in Oliver," says Ray. "Its neglected vineyard was selling grapes in quantity rather than using a more disciplined farming technique for quality. I had travelled the wine country of Europe in my bachelor years and knew quite precisely the personality and characteristics I envisioned in the wines I loved reinterpreted here on this terroir. The first time I saw the vineyard unfolding from the kitchen window, I felt that the foot of the vineyard would make a perfect location for a small family winery."

Luckily, Catherine shared the vino vision. As her career was taking a turn, she dove into wine studies in Montreal. She joined the family caravan heading to wine country and is now happily crafting wines alongside her dad. Nathalie was living her own dream as an artist in Vancouver when her now husband Sean Donelan was transferred to Oliver to work on a project. She relocated, and the two were married on the vineyard. Nathalie's art career is thriving, with her work hanging in galleries across the country as well as on the walls of the winery's tasting lounge.

Coulombe Family Tourtière

This beloved family recipe for a French Canadian–style meat pie, a signature dish in Quebec, is a Christmas Eve tradition in the Coulombe home. This recipe has evolved from the one Ray Coulombe's maman made for him on the farm when he was growing up. Instead of ground meat, "hers featured wonderful cubes of whatever farmed and hunted meats were available at the time," Ray remembers. On Christmas Eve, when his family returned from midnight Mass, they would sit down to devour the tourtière fresh out of the oven before retiring to bed with full bellies, ready for presents late the next morning. The pie crust recipe makes enough for two single-crust pies or one double-crust pie.

Serves 6–8

Pie Crust:

1 cup unsalted butter, chilled and cut into small pieces

2½ cups chilled flour

1 tsp salt

1 tsp sugar

½ cup ice water

For the Pie Crust:

Line a baking sheet with parchment paper and lay out ¾ cup of the butter pieces on it. Place the sheet in the freezer until the butter is hard, about 30 minutes. Put the remaining butter in the fridge.

In a food processor, combine the flour, salt and sugar. Add the butter from the fridge and pulse to combine, about 10 times. Add the frozen butter and pulse until the mixture is coarse with some blueberry-size clumps.

Tourtière:

1 lb ground veal

1 lb ground pork

1 medium onion, finely chopped

2 cloves garlic, minced

1 tsp salt, or to taste

½ tsp pepper

½ tsp ground cloves

½ tsp ground cinnamon

¼ tsp dry mustard

1 cup (or less) breadcrumbs

1 recipe pie crust or 2 premade deep-dish pie crusts (one each for top and bottom)

1 egg, beaten

Note: Family secret: swap ¼ cup of the ice water in the crust for chilled vodka!

Pair with: vinAmité Compass Bordeaux blend. The aromas of savoury dark chocolate and rich latte bring you front and centre to the taste of blackcurrant, blueberry, black cherry, nutmeg, clove, mocha and leather, all rolled into a nice bundle of confident tannins.

Add the ice water and immediately pulse until the water is just incorporated, about 10 times. To test if the pastry is ready, squeeze a small amount of dough between your fingers to make sure it holds together. If it doesn't, pulse a few more times.

Lay out two pieces of plastic wrap. Divide the dough in half and set each piece in the middle of a piece of plastic wrap. Draw the edges together to gather the dough into a bundle, and press to form into two discs.

Roll out the discs, still wrapped in plastic wrap, until they are ½-inch-thick rounds, 8 inches in diameter. Refrigerate for at least 45 minutes and up to 2 days, or freeze for up to 1 month.

For the Tourtière:

Preheat the oven to 425°F.

In a large saucepan over medium-high heat, place the meat, onions, garlic, spices and ¼ cup of water (if the meat is dry and there is not much liquid in the pan, add up to 1 cup water). Bring to a slow boil, then quickly lower the heat. Simmer for up to 30 minutes, uncovered, to let the spices permeate the meats.

Remove from heat and add the breadcrumbs a few spoonfuls at a time, stirring to absorb the leftover juices. Let the mixture stand for about 5 minutes between additions, then stir to see if more breadcrumbs are required. Only add enough to absorb the juices—too many breadcrumbs will dry out the mixture.

Line a pie plate with one pie crust and fill the shell with the meat mixture, heaping the filling gradually higher toward the centre.

Lay the second pie crust overtop and seal by fluting the edges. Brush the crust with egg wash. Do not cut vents. Bake until the top crust is an appealing brown, about 30 minutes.

Hester Creek Estate Winery

www.hestercreek.com
877 Road 8, Oliver

In a glorious setting on Oliver's hillside, Hester Creek Estate Winery has stood the test of time in the Oliver grape industry. The stone and granite tasting bar extends to a private dining area and a professional demonstration kitchen. This is where Roger Gillespie, the charming and gracious director of hospitality at Hester Creek, (along with visiting chefs and instructors) captivates his food- and wine-loving audience at cooking classes.

Hester Creek is home to some of the oldest vines in the entire BC wine industry, planted in 1968 by the property's original owner, visionary Joe Busnardo. Joe was one of the first to plant European *Vitis vinifera* cuttings, which he brought from his homeland in northern Italy. He knew this area had the perfect conditions to grow excellent grapes; what he didn't know at the time was that one day the region would become known as the Golden Mile Bench, with a reputation for excellent wines.

Joe's early success encouraged him to plant over 80 classic European *vinifera* grapes on the then 76-acre property. Today, his Pinot Blanc, Trebbiano, Merlot and Cabernet Franc continue to thrive on Hester Creek's now 115-acre estate. "We are honoured to be a steward of these rare old vines," says Hester Creek Estate Winery president Mark Sheridan. "The risk-taking spirit of the early BC wine pioneers is something we are proud to be a part of."

Proprietor Curt Garland, a Prince George entrepreneur and humanitarian, purchased the Hester Creek Estate property in 2004 and breathed new life into it with an inspired Mediterranean vision for the future. He hired veteran winemaker Rob Summers from Niagara to finesse the stellar fruit grown on the estate and bring it to its current multi-award-winning glory. Rob also helped create the meticulously designed 23,000-square-foot winery.

The estate also includes Terrafina, a charming Tuscan-style restaurant. Operated by the award-winning restaurateur team RauDZ Creative Concepts, Terrafina crafts farm-to-table Italian-style cuisine. The terrace features some of the original grapevines from the 1968 planting. Visitors who plan to linger can book a room at the luxurious Mediterranean villa–style accommodations built atop the hillside.

Roger's 3-Day Braised Pork-Rib Spaghetti

This rich Italian braised meat sauce is all about the length of time you patiently simmer the sauce. It really does take 3 days! Hester Creek's chef and director of hospitality, Roger Gillespie, first enjoyed a version of this sauce at an elderly Italian gentleman's home in 2002, paired with an aged bottle of Brunello di Montalcino. Roger's friend was kind enough to share his secrets, and ever since, Roger's family has enjoyed his own version. This is also Hester Creek owner Curt Garland's favourite dish, and Roger makes it for him when he is in town.

This is a big recipe and makes about 16 cups of sauce. It can be halved, but the results are better if you go all out so that there is enough liquid to slow-cook the ribs—and if you're cooking for 3 days, you may as well make lots! The sauce can be stored for 3–4 days in the fridge or up to 6 months in the freezer.

Serves about 18

2 large sweet onions (preferably Walla Walla), diced

¼ cup olive oil

1 head garlic, minced

6 stalks celery with leaves, diced

1 cup tomato paste

2 tsp cayenne

2 cups quality white wine

2 cups chicken stock

5 lb tomatoes, cored and diced

4 full racks pork ribs (side or back), cut into 1- to 2-bone pieces

6 (each 796 ml/28 oz) cans Pomodoro della Sardegna (see note)

2–3 Parmesan cheese rinds

½ cup demerara sugar

Salt and pepper

Balsamic reduction, for seasoning (optional)

Spaghetti, to serve

Grated Parmesan, to serve

Garlic toast, to serve (optional)

In a 20-quart stockpot, sauté the onions in the oil over medium heat until translucent, about 10 minutes. Add the garlic, celery, tomato paste and cayenne and sauté for another minute.

Deglaze with the white wine and reduce by half.

Add the chicken stock and then the diced tomatoes and simmer for 10 minutes. Add the ribs, 2–3 cans of tomatoes (enough to cover the ribs) and the Parmesan rinds. Bring the entire pot to a low simmer, then lower the heat to medium-low to keep it at a very slow simmer. The mixture should be barely bubbling.

During the day, every hour or so, check the pot, stir and ensure the ribs are still submerged. If the liquid levels drop too low, add a can of tomatoes and their juice. Continue this process over the next 2 days. If your kitchen isn't set up for overnight cooking, simmer the sauce for 10–12 hours, cool it and refrigerate overnight. Then repeat the process on day two. Late into day two, you may notice the bones dissipating into the sauce. This is expected.

By midday on day three, you can remove any remaining bones— but do not be surprised if there are not many or even none. Begin the seasoning process by adding the sugar, salt and pepper and, if you like, the balsamic reduction, which brings some depth to the sauce and possibly a touch of sweetness to balance out the acidity. The level of sweetness desired is a personal thing, so you decide. Taste and adjust seasoning as needed.

Note: If you can't find Pomodoro della Sardegna, you can use any good Italian plum tomatoes. Casar is a good brand from Italy.

Serve over a good-quality Italian spaghetti, topped with freshly grated Parmesan, with a slice of garlic toast. And now is your chance to yell loudly, Lidia Bastianich–style: "*Tutti a tavola a mangiare!*" (Everyone to the table to eat!)

Pair with: Hester Creek 2016 Garland. From a superior vintage, this elegant old-vines Cabernet-dominant blend shows immediate aromas of dark cherry with subtle undertones of cedar, clove, vanilla, sage and fresh-cut alfalfa.

CheckMate Artisanal Winery

www.checkmatewinery.com
4799 Wild Rose Street, Oliver

CheckMate Artisanal Winery is a marvel. One of the famed Anthony von Mandl wineries, CheckMate has chosen two varietals to create in their highest forms: Chardonnay and Merlot. The winery makes several versions of each to demonstrate the power of terroir.

"The Installation, a Pop-up by Tom Kundig" winery concept is thrilling. Like a glass box sitting atop the vineyards overlooking Oliver below, the tasting room is the very first of its kind. Tasters enjoy the benefits of full roll-back windows in appropriate weather, allowing a rare opportunity for a proper open-air tasting experience. On cooler days, the windows provide the illusion of being outdoors and communing with the nature surrounding the tasting bar. A new tasting room and renovated winery are to come, but for now, we can enjoy this treat.

For Chardonnay fans, this is a haven, and for wine geeks, an opportunity to taste a range of wines, including one featuring the vines that brought forth the Top Chardonnay in the World award at the International Wine & Spirit Competition in London in 1994. This award winner was the catalyst for Anthony von Mandl to begin plans for this exclusive winery.

Hailing from Australia, Phil McGahan is a lawyer turned winemaker with an utter dedication to making sophisticated Chardonnay and Merlot. His approach includes "meticulously focusing on small, family-owned and -farmed estate vineyards, and relentlessly studying and researching rows within them to define micro blocks." As winemaker, he unleashes the natural potential of his wines by trusting in the absolute purity, complexity and quality of the grapes they are made from. He uses no fining methods or filtration.

The theme of the winery, if you hadn't guessed, is the game of chess. The seven Chardonnays include Capture, Queen Taken, Queen's Advantage, Knight's Challenge, Attack, Little Pawn and Fool's Mate, and the four different expressions of Merlot are Black Rook, End Game, Opening Gambit and Silent Bishop.

In both cases, the vineyards that the wines are sourced from are all meticulously tended by hand. CheckMate is a lesson in both terroir and excellence.

Florence's Tarragon Chicken

CheckMate winemaker Phil McGahan grew up in Western Queensland, Australia, as the youngest of 10 children. His parents, Jack and Florence, supported their large brood by raising their own chickens and keeping a quarter-acre vegetable garden. "Most Saturday mornings, my dad and I would kill and dress two chickens for our family's dinner. One of my mom's specialties was this tarragon chicken recipe, made with fresh tarragon picked from my dad's vegetable garden. The licorice character of the tarragon was always a great pairing with the chicken. This dish is deeply connected to the land I grew up on and makes the perfect post-harvest celebration."

Serves 4

1 (3½ lb) free-range chicken
Salt and pepper
4 Tbsp chopped tarragon leaves, plus additional to garnish
¼ cup butter
1 clove garlic, minced
⅔ cup chicken stock
⅔ cup CheckMate Little Pawn Chardonnay
1 Tbsp flour
⅔ cup cream
Chive blossoms, to garnish (optional)

Pair with: CheckMate Little Pawn Chardonnay. This wine has a captivating floral nose with hints of rose petal, cinnamon spice and lemon zest. On the palate, subtle richness, hints of cream and a beautiful oak integration create a wine of restrained elegance with substantial length.

Preheat the oven to 390°F.

Pat the chicken dry with paper towel and season with salt.

Mix 3 Tbsp of the tarragon with half of the butter and the garlic, and season with salt and pepper. Form into a ball and insert into the bird cavity.

In an oven-safe pot or Dutch oven over low heat, melt the remaining butter. Brown the chicken on all sides, then remove it from the pot and set aside. Add the chicken stock and wine to the pot and simmer for 1–2 minutes to evaporate the alcohol. Return the chicken to the pot, cover and roast in the oven for 80 minutes or until the juices run clear when the thigh is pierced with a skewer.

Remove the chicken to a plate, holding it over the pot to allow all the juices to drain into the pot. Cover the chicken with a tea towel and allow to rest.

Skim most of the surface fat from the juices in the pot, leaving about 1 Tbsp. Return the pot to the stove over medium-high heat and mix in the flour, whisking quickly, until the sauce boils and thickens.

Strain the sauce into a clean saucepan and add the remaining tarragon. Simmer for about 2 minutes, then stir in the cream. Season with salt and pepper and heat without allowing it to boil.

To serve, carve the chicken and spoon the sauce overtop. Top with more tarragon and fresh chive blossoms, if you like.

Desert Hills Estate Winery

www.deserthills.ca
4078 Black Sage Road, Oliver

French novelist Antoine de Saint-Exupéry once wrote, "What makes the desert beautiful is that somewhere it hides a well." At Desert Hills Estate Winery, that "well" bestows amazing wine.

Located on Oliver's vineyard-rich Black Sage Road (which is almost like a Wine Walk of Fame), Desert Hills and its neighbouring wineries sit on some of the finest terroir in the valley. The three Toor brothers opened the winery in 2003 with a then 24-acre vineyard appropriately named Three Boys Vineyard. Before that, the land was an apple orchard.

Twin brothers Randy and Jessie and their younger brother Dave operate this major award-winning winery. Randy focuses on the business side of the winery, growing the grapes and overseeing the winemaking process, and Jessie manages the vineyards. Winemaker Anthony Buchanan works closely with the family.

Randy's son Rajen has joined the family business too, and is creating his own small production label called Ursa Major Estate Winery. Learning firsthand from his father and uncles, Rajen has been thoroughly educated in the winemaking industry from vine to bottle, as well as marketing. He will one day become the winemaker for all of their labels.

The Toor family all live in a big house on-site, and the Toor women lovingly prepare and cook the daily meals for their family with ingredients from Grandma Sukhminder's vegetable and herb garden on the estate. Wanting to share their passion for delicious, healthy Indian food with the community, they recently opened the Black Sage Bistro on the vineyard with Executive Chef Patrick Khatri at the helm. A longtime family friend, Patrick has created a menu that features some of the family's house favourites along with his own interpretive Indian dishes. The views from this property are supernatural—there are certain times of day when the sunlight paints the vineyard in gold and it literally glows against the desert mountains.

Desert Hills is known for its big reds, and its flagship Bordeaux blend, Mirage, is a huge critic favourite. The team also makes a port-style wine, five white wines and a rosé.

Toor Family Black Lentil Dal

This is one of the Toor family's favourites, made by Lakhwinder Toor. Chef Patrick Khatri of Desert Hills Winery's Black Sage Bistro has come up with measurements for this cookbook, but says, "The beautiful part about this dish is that there are no measurements—it's all based on feeling and love. The more lentils you use, the more of everything else you'll need, and you can also play around with your spice levels and, of course, consistency. To make it creamier, cook longer. More runny, cook less. It's all about essences and intuition. Don't be shy, and put your own spin on this warm, healthy, nourishing dish."

Serves 4

3 cups black lentils (beluga lentils), thoroughly washed

2 tsp vegetable oil

½ white onion, finely diced

2 cloves garlic, minced

1 tsp minced ginger

1 tsp cumin seeds

1 tsp salt

½ tsp ground turmeric

1 tsp additional spices of your choice (try minced green chilies or chili powder)

¼ cup chopped cilantro, to garnish

In a saucepan, bring 4 cups of water to a boil, then add the lentils. Boil, covered, until just tender, up to 1 hour.

While the lentils are cooking, prepare the *tadka* (the finishing spices). In a nonstick pan over medium heat, heat the vegetable oil and then add the onions, garlic, ginger and cumin seeds. Sauté until just before they start to turn golden brown, about 3 minutes. Add the salt, turmeric and additional spices and sauté until the mixture is golden brown, about 3–4 minutes.

When the lentils are tender, stir in the tadka and simmer for another 15–20 minutes. Taste and adjust salt and spice to your liking. Garnish with the cilantro and serve.

Pair with: Desert Hills Gamay Noir. Lakhwinder's favourite wine, this is a rich and complex Gamay with notes of raspberry and dark cherry complemented by leathery and earthy tones.

Burrowing Owl Estate Winery

www.burrowingowlwine.ca
500 Burrowing Owl Place (off Black Sage Road), Oliver

Backdropped by desert rock mountains and wrapped in terraces for enjoying the dramatic views, Burrowing Owl Estate Winery has created one of the most captivating viewpoints on Oliver's Black Sage Road and captures the full magic of wine country.

The winery's fine-dining restaurant, the Sonora Room, offers a warm European-style room and terrace tables that share the glamorous view. There is a well-appointed inn, event facilities and a pool to lounge beside after a long, hard day of wine tasting.

With one of the most recognizable wine labels in the industry, Burrowing Owl has been a go-to brand for decades. Looking for a retirement project in his mid-50s, owner Jim Wyse stumbled across the 100-acre property, which was in need of great repair. He and wife Midge couldn't resist. From day one, the family took a kind of Hippocratic oath ("to do no harm") with respect to the environment. They take the care and stewardship of one of Canada's most unique ecosystems very seriously, and that extends to all of the viticulture and oenological practices at Burrowing Owl.

"Jim's mother's love of birds influenced the naming of the property," explains Midge. "There was a property across the road where there had been an attempt to re-establish this endangered bird. This led to a membership and directorship in the Burrowing Owl Conservation Society and long-term support that continues to this day."

Because the entire business is family-run, it has a special charm and warmth. Son Chris Wyse is president of the winery, and daughter Kerri Wyse-McNolty handles marketing. Son Stephen moved to the Okanagan with his partner, Michelle Young, in 1996 and trained under original winemaker Bill Dyer to make Burrowing Owl's first on-site wines in 1998. The couple managed the day-to-day operations until 2006, when they purchased their own Osoyoos property, the Young & Wyse Collection.

The burrowing owl is an endangered desert species indigenous to the Oliver area. The support of the Wyse family has helped fund a conservation centre, complete with an in-house scientist to help educate people about this little owl and protect its species.

Pair with: Burrowing Owl Chardonnay. Ripe fruit nicely integrated with oak offers notes of vanilla, popcorn, white peach and lemon on the nose. It has a creamy palate followed by crisp, juicy acidity.

Seared Arctic Char with Parsley Crust, Roasted Eggplant & Zucchini

Burrowing Owl Estate Winery's Midge Wyse is an avid cook who loves to entertain, and works with the Sonora Room chef to take some of her dishes to the next level—like this one, which she created with Chef Lee Humphries. She makes this dish with Arctic char from Road 17, a sustainable fish farm in Oliver.

Serves 4

Parsley Crust:

2 cups finely chopped flat-leaf parsley

½ cup butter, room temperature

1 clove garlic, minced

¼ cup breadcrumbs

2 heaping Tbsp grated Parmesan cheese

Salt and pepper

Sauce:

1 cup white wine

4 Tbsp unsalted butter

1 Tbsp chopped herbs, such as tarragon or basil

Salt and pepper

Fish & Roasted Vegetables:

2 Japanese eggplants, sliced into rounds and halved if large

2 zucchini, sliced into rounds and halved if large

3 Tbsp olive oil

Salt and pepper

4 (each 6 oz) fillets Arctic char

Fresh microgreens or edible flowers of your choice (optional)

For the Parsley Crust:

Purée the parsley, butter and garlic together in a food processor until smooth. Gradually add the breadcrumbs and Parmesan cheese, and season with salt and pepper.

Place between two sheets of parchment paper and roll out into a ⅓-inch-thick sheet. Refrigerate until cold and easy to slice, about 20 minutes. Remove from the fridge and cut into portions sized to match the fish fillets. Set aside.

For the Sauce:

In a saucepan over medium-high heat, reduce the wine by half. Lower the heat and whisk in the butter. Stir in the herbs and season with salt and pepper. Set aside.

For the Fish & Roasted Vegetables:

Preheat the oven to 400°F.

Brush the eggplant and zucchini rounds with 1 Tbsp of the olive oil, then sprinkle with salt and pepper. Grill until just softened, but still firm, and keep warm.

In an oven-safe frying pan over medium heat, heat the remaining olive oil. Add the fish fillets and sear until golden on one side. Flip the portions and top each with a matching slab of parsley crust. Move the pan to the oven and bake until the fish is cooked, about 4 minutes.

Serve each fillet with grilled vegetables, atop a layer of sauce. Top with fresh microgreens or edible flowers, if you like.

Nk'Mip Cellars

www.nkmipcellars.com
1400 Rancher Creek Road, Osoyoos

The first Indigenous-owned winery in North America, Nk'Mip (pronounced in-KA-meep) Cellars sits majestically atop Spirit Ridge in the desert mountains of Osoyoos. First to greet you as you wind your way up the hillside to the winery is a beautiful sculpture of an Indigenous warrior, arms raised to the skies, with a dramatic backdrop of the valley below. You will *feel* this land and, if you listen closely, you might hear a whispering from the past and the centuries of footprints that lie beneath you.

Nk'Mip Cellars is a cultural celebration of the Osoyoos Indian Band and testament to the innovation of Chief Clarence Louie. He had a vision and dream to plant vineyards and build a winery, and he brought that vision to life in 2002. The winery represents a joint venture between the Osoyoos Indian Band (Syilx People) and Arterra Wines Canada.

Nk'Mip Cellars towers over the shimmering Osoyoos Lake below, with vineyards skirting around it. The winery is set among a village that includes a golf course, a market, restaurants, Spirit Ridge Resort (operated by Hyatt Hotels) and the Nk'Mip Desert Cultural Centre, which is operated by the Osoyoos Indian Band and provides a fascinating look at the Band's history, lands, legends and people. The winery's patio restaurant has an incredible view and offers Indigenous-inspired, locally sourced farm-to-table cuisine.

Winemaker Justin Hall is a proud member of the Osoyoos Indian Band, and the first Indigenous winemaker in North America (and maybe even the world). He is passionate about creating wines and in love with his craft. Justin grew up on the Oliver land reservation, and once he was exposed to the world of winemaking by the head winemaker at Nk'Mip Cellars, Randy Picton, his destiny was set. Randy has been at the winery since its creation and built the repertoire of wines. He has been a wonderful mentor for Justin and created an atmosphere for him to shine.

As Canada's only "pocket desert," Osoyoos has a unique ecosystem. Justin grew up in the area, foraging and hunting, and has extraordinary knowledge of all the plants and animals on this land and in its waters. This gives him special insights into the unique terroir of the wines they are creating.

The winery creates three wine labels: the Winemakers Tier, Qwam Qwmt and Mer'r'iym. Their repertoire includes an array of red and white wines, blends and an icewine.

Justin's Crispy-Skin Sockeye Salmon with Saskatoon Berry Sauce

Osoyoos Lake is an extraordinary spawning ground for sockeye salmon thanks to the work done by the Okanagan Nation Alliance (ONA) to reopen the natural waterways for the salmon to return as they did decades ago. The ONA has a dedicated group of fishers who use the same holistic traditional practices during fish harvest as their ancestors did. They return certain parts of the salmon to the river of origin during fish harvest, and offer portions of fish to eagles and owls. This reinforces the strong reciprocal bonds within the broader ecosystem and their beliefs and deep bond with nature. Sockeye salmon play an integral role in Indigenous culture, not only as a regular food source but also as a cultural and spiritual icon.

This recipe comes from Nk'Mip Cellars winemaker Justin Hall. An avid fisher and forager, he also happens to be an excellent cook.

Serves 4

Saskatoon Berry Sauce:

2 cups Saskatoon berries, fresh or frozen (see note)

½ cup sugar

1 tsp pure vanilla

1 stick cinnamon

2 pods star anise

2 tsp cornstarch

Salmon:

4 (each 6 oz) skin-on fillets wild BC sockeye salmon

Sea salt and pepper

1 Tbsp vegetable, canola or light olive oil

1 Tbsp butter

Notes: If you can't find Saskatoon berries, you can use blueberries instead. The sauce is delicious and would also work well on cheesecake or ice cream or as a condiment for venison.

For the Saskatoon Berry Sauce:

Place the berries, sugar, vanilla, cinnamon stick and star anise in a saucepan over low heat. Bring to a simmer and reduce by one-quarter.

In a small bowl, mix the cornstarch with ½ cup water, then whisk into the berry mixture to thicken. Simmer for another 2 minutes, then remove from heat and discard the cinnamon and star anise. This sauce can be made in advance. It keeps for a week in the fridge and up to 3 months in the freezer.

For the Salmon:

Press the salmon fillets between paper towel to dry the surfaces thoroughly. Sprinkle with salt and pepper to evenly coat the top and bottom. The seasoning here is key, as the crispy skin is a part of the finished dish.

In a large frying pan, heat the oil and butter over medium-high heat until shimmering. Lower the heat to medium-low, then add a salmon fillet, skin side down. Press firmly in place for 10 seconds, using the back of a flexible fish spatula, to prevent the skin from buckling.

Add the remaining fillets one at a time, pressing each with the spatula for 10 seconds, until all the fillets are in the pan.

Cook, pressing gently on the back of the fillets occasionally to ensure good contact with the skin, until the skin releases easily from the pan, about 4 minutes. If the skin shows resistance when

continued

you attempt to lift a corner with the spatula, continue to cook until it lifts easily. Continue to cook until the salmon registers 110°F in the very centre for rare, 120°F for medium-rare or 130°F for medium, another 5–7 minutes total.

Justin does not flip his salmon fillets unless they are quite thick. If you would like to flip them, use a spatula and a fork to turn them over and cook on the second side for 15 seconds. Transfer the fillets to a paper towel–lined plate to drain. Serve immediately, on a bed of microgreens and tomatoes if you like, with a side of Saskatoon berry sauce.

Pair with: Nk'Mip Rosé. With aromas of cherry, grapefruit and wild berries, and a palate that has an intense fruit explosion of grapefruit and red berry, this wine is clean and crisp with just enough sweetness to balance out the palate, which leads to a mouth-watering finish.

Moon Curser Vineyards

www.mooncurser.com
3628 Highway 3 East, Osoyoos

An interesting name for a winery, Moon Curser conjures an air of thrilling mysticism. It's the same kind of feeling you get when standing on the edge of the Moon Curser vineyards, marvelling at the desert views of Osoyoos below. Maybe you are feeling the energy from the past—these vineyards have a wonderfully clandestine history of gold smugglers tiptoeing over the border. Or perhaps it is the wonderful energy of owners Chris and Beata Tolley, an enterprising couple with a great sense of adventure and a shared passion for making wine.

"Moon curser" is a synonym for "smuggler"—a fitting name for a winery in the hills of the border town of Osoyoos (below the appropriately named Anarchist Mountain), which was a hotspot for smuggling during the gold rush years. "We find it's such a lovely way to tie back into the whole concept of terroir and have the name speak to where we grow our wine," says Beata. "We could never grow grapes like Tannat or Dolcetto if we were not located at the southernmost tip of the Okanagan, Canada's hotspot." Yes, this is a fun brand . . . with seriously amazing wines.

Beata was born in Gdańsk in Poland and moved to Calgary with her family when she was 16. Chris grew up in Montreal and moved to Calgary at about the same age. The two met in a calculus class and ended up in very un-wine-like careers. Beata explains, "I ended up becoming a chartered accountant and Chris a civil engineer/software designer." The two were happily living in Alberta when, like many, they became captivated by the idea of making wine and living the vineyard life, so they packed up and moved to New Zealand to submerse themselves in the wine culture and complete post-graduate degrees in viticulture and oenology at Lincoln University in Christchurch.

In 2004 they took the plunge and purchased an old orchard and fruit stand on Highway 3 in Osoyoos, then set about transforming it into a vineyard and winery. Beata says, "We were attracted to our property, and to the Osoyoos East Bench in general, because it is a beautiful Class 1 grapegrowing area. We were planning on planting grape varieties that had not been previously farmed in the Okanagan (Tannat, Tempranillo, etc.) and wanted to make sure that we were situated in the best possible spot for successful viticultural adventuring. It also didn't hurt that Osoyoos turned out to be a small, lovely and welcoming community with a long history of farming fruits and vegetables. We immediately felt at home and have made many lifelong friends in the community."

Plum Clafoutis

Clafoutis is a traditional baked French dessert that sounds intimidating but is actually very easy. Moon Curser Vineyards' Beata Tolley, who is busy with a winery and two young children, says that this dessert is on regular rotation in their house, especially during summer and fall months when the abundant Okanagan fruit is at its best. Plum is a favourite in this recipe because of its lovely tartness, but feel free to experiment with other Okanagan fruits like cherries, peaches, grapes and apricots. A super kid-friendly dish, clafoutis makes for a wonderful breakfast or after-school snack.

Serves 6–8

1¼ cups milk

3 eggs

⅔ cup sugar

½ cup flour

1 Tbsp pure vanilla

Pinch of salt

3 cups chopped pitted plums (bite-size pieces)

Icing sugar, for dusting

Ice cream or whipped cream, to serve (optional)

Note: If you are lucky enough to have a wood-fired oven, this dish makes the perfect finale after a couple of rounds of pizzas. Beata says, "[My father-in-law] Monty's wood-fire oven is a great gathering place for friends and family alike."

Preheat the oven to 350°F. Lightly grease a 9-inch baking dish casserole dish or cast-iron frying pan.

In a blender, combine the milk, eggs, ⅓ cup of the sugar, and the flour, vanilla and salt. Blend on high for about 1 minute.

Pour a ¼-inch layer of the blended mixture over the bottom of the baking dish and set the remaining batter aside.

Bake until a film starts to form on the batter and it starts to firm up a little, about 5 minutes.

Remove the dish from the oven and scatter the chopped plums overtop. Pour the remaining batter over the plums, and sprinkle with the remaining sugar.

Return to the oven and bake until the clafoutis is puffed and golden brown and a knife inserted into the centre of the topping comes out clean, about 45–60 minutes.

Remove from the oven and dust with icing sugar. Serve warm with or without vanilla ice cream or whipped cream.

Pair with: Moon Curser Dolcetto. Best served slightly chilled, this medium-bodied wine has a deep ruby, garnet colour. On the nose you will find notes of prunes, cherries and dark spices. On the palate, blackberries take the lead along with the almond notes typical of Dolcetto.

Forbidden Fruit Winery

www.forbiddenfruitwine.com
620 Sumac Road, Cawston

both of their children are involved in the business, as are their children's spouses. "We never thought that our children would be part of what we do," says Kim, "but they both grew up on a farm and obviously recognized the value of the lifestyle. There is something to say about sharing a special bond when you work with your children." Kim is also a fabulous artist, and the tasting room doubles as a gallery featuring her works.

Across from the tasting room is a stand where they sell their organic fruit literally in the orchard. Above that, a log-cabin guesthouse is available to rent if you fancy a full immersion into their magical organic world.

Kim and Steve started Ven'Amour Organic Farms (a romantic combination of their last names) in 1977. Steve was one of the first growers to join the organic farm movement. For over 40 years, the farm has been producing organic fruit on this secluded property, and the result is beautiful, clean fruit and grapes that create outstanding wines. The family also sells their products at farmers' markets around BC.

S nuggled on the banks of the rugged Similkameen River in Cawston, Forbidden Fruit Winery and Ven'Amour Organic Farms is a 38-acre certified organic family farm set within a 142-acre nature estate. It feels like a modern-day Garden of Eden—a comparison that inspired the name of the winery. The views as you enter the valley are staggering, especially in the fall, when the colours are electric.

Owners Steve Venables and Kim Brind'Amour are a treat to visit. The winery is a family affair:

Their flagship fruit wines include sparkling and dessert wines, but they also produce the Earth Series and Dead End grape wines, as well as fruit ciders. In 2015 Forbidden Fruit was the first-ever winery in the Pacific Northwest to win top medals in both the grape wine and the fruit wine categories in the same competition.

Porter's Favourite Chocolate Pear Cake

Pears and chocolate? Yes, please! Teshia Marven (daughter of Forbidden Fruit's owners) is the baker in the family, and she created this beautiful cake, which is a favourite of *her* daughter, Porter Amour. It just keeps getting better a day or two after you make it—if it lasts that long!

Serves 8

Cake:

⅓ cup + 1 Tbsp butter

4 oz dark chocolate, chopped into small pieces (reserving some for garnish)

½ cup Forbidden Fruit Impearfection dessert wine

6 organic Anjou pears, peeled, halved and cored (or enough to fill bottom of a 9-inch cake pan)

1½ cups organic flour

½ cup organic sugar

1 tsp baking powder

1 tsp baking soda

¼ tsp salt

2 eggs

½ cup milk

1 tsp pure vanilla

⅓ cup mayonnaise

Icing:

¼ cup cream cheese, room temperature

¼ cup honey

Assembly:

Dark chocolate shavings

Note: If you like, double the icing recipe—it is delicious!

For the Cake:

Preheat the oven to 350°F. Grease a 9-inch cake pan and set aside.

In a small saucepan, melt ⅓ cup of the butter and the chocolate. Stir together and set aside.

In a large frying pan, melt 1 Tbsp of the butter. Add the wine and pears and cook for 5–10 minutes, until still slightly firm. Set aside.

Mix the dry ingredients in a bowl. In another bowl, lightly whisk the eggs, then add the milk and vanilla. Slowly add the dry ingredients to the wet ingredients and mix together. Add the mayonnaise and the melted chocolate and butter mixture, stirring to combine.

Arrange the pear halves in the cake pan, flat side down with the stem ends facing in and the pears touching. Pour in the cake batter, and shake the pan to distribute evenly.

Bake for 30–35 minutes, or until a toothpick inserted in the centre of the cake comes out clean. Allow to cool completely in the pan.

For the Icing:

With a whisk or mixer, whip the cream cheese and honey until the mixture reaches a pourable consistency. To make the cream cheese easier to whip, put it in the microwave for a few seconds to soften.

For Assembly:

Turn the cake out onto a serving plate so that the pears show on top. Drizzle with the icing and garnish with pear and chocolate.

Pair with: Forbidden Fruit Winery Impearfection Asian Pear Dessert Wine. A white semi-sweet wine made from organic Asian pears. The pear aromas and flavours are accompanied by notes of ginger, papaya, lychee, and wildflower honey. Serve chilled.

Little Farm Winery

www.littlefarmwinery.ca
2155 Newton Road, Cawston

Alishan Driediger is a renaissance woman: baker, grocer, farmer, crafter, maverick winemaker, fabulous cook, pet rescuer, mom and the kindest superwoman you will ever meet.

Little Farm Winery is located in Cawston, the kind of small town that country songs are written about. "It's like the Wild West, with cowboys on horseback doing cattle roundups and everything!" says Alishan. "It's a pretty eclectic and interesting community that includes farmers, winemakers, ranchers, artists, musicians, hippies, draft dodgers and lots of younger people and families getting into organic farming. There is definitely a sense of community and that we are all in it together here, especially in our little wine industry. Everyone knows each other and helps each other, lends out equipment . . .

"I love that we are surrounded by tons of organic food, good wine, and clean air and fresh water from the ground. It's a great place to grow grapes! The valley, the river, the soils, the crazy intense desert sun, cool nights, insane wind . . . it all makes for pretty special fruit!" Little Farm produces only single-vineyard wine made with minimal intervention to reflect the terroir.

Alishan's passion for the food and wine industry was born while she was travelling in the South of France in her early 20s. She received a professional culinary diploma, then branched out to farming and studied agricultural sciences, becoming interested in wine. She and partner Rhys Pender purchased Little Farm and planted a vineyard, then Alishan jumped into the winemaking program at University of California, Davis.

One of the perks of operating a small winery is the ability to experiment with some really cool winemaking techniques. Alishan has been working with wild natural ferments, or *Pied de Cuve* (natural wines), something she learned in France. "We pick a small bin of grapes, then stomp/crush them in the vineyard and then leave the bin there in the vines to start fermenting. It's kind of like a sourdough starter. Once the bin is fermenting, it can be used as a starter to kick off the fermentation for a tank of wine." Stay tuned for exciting news of a sparkling wine and a tasting room in the future.

Choucroute Garni

This is the ultimate crowd-pleasing comfort food. The aromas wafting from your kitchen will draw crowds—especially of people who have visited Alsace, where this dish is queen of comfort. Basically, sauerkraut, potatoes and a variety of delicious smoked things like sausages, ham and bacon all cook together in a big old pot of love with a bottle of wine added to further enhance the hedonism. Alishan Driediger began this feast tradition as an annual Beaujolais Nouveau party, but when she began making her own wine, it morphed into a Riesling party to celebrate the flagship wine of Little Farm Winery.

Serves 10–12

5 lb sauerkraut, drained

25 black peppercorns

15 juniper berries

1½ tsp coriander seeds

5 whole cloves

6 sprigs flat-leaf parsley

4 sprigs thyme

2 bay leaves

½ cup duck fat or peanut oil

4 medium onions, sliced ⅛-inch thick

1 bottle Riesling or other dry white wine

2 cups chicken stock

2½ lb smoked bacon

1½ lb slab dry-salted bacon, rinsed and dried (see note)

2 lb smoked pork butt

2 dry-salted pig's knuckles (about 1½ lb)

10 carrots, peeled

¼ cup finely minced garlic

2 tsp salt

10–15 small red potatoes

8 white veal sausages (weisswurst or bockwurst)

8 smoked country sausages (bauerwurst)

8 knackwurst sausages

Place the sauerkraut in a colander in the sink. Rinse with warm water and drain.

Make a bouquet garni: place the peppercorns, juniper berries, coriander seeds, cloves, parsley, thyme and bay leaves on a square of cheesecloth, then bundle and tie the top together with kitchen twine.

Melt the duck fat in a very large Dutch oven or heavy stockpot over medium heat (you may need to use two pots). Add the onions and sauté for about 10 minutes or until translucent. Add the wine, chicken stock and 2 cups of water and stir. Add both bacons, the pork butt, pig's knuckles, carrots, garlic and salt.

Add the bouquet garni, then pile the sauerkraut on top of the mixture and add enough cold water to bring the liquid to 1 inch below the sauerkraut. Cover, increase the heat to high and bring the liquid to a boil. Turn the heat to medium-low and cook at a strong simmer until the meat is almost falling off the bone and the fat is rendered from the slab of bacon, about 1½ hours.

Add the potatoes and cook for 20–30 minutes, or until they are almost fork-tender. Add all the sausages, cover and simmer until they are heated through, another 10 minutes or so.

To serve, remove the bouquet garni. Slice the slab of bacon and the pork butt. Using tongs, arrange the meat, potatoes, carrots and drained sauerkraut on a large platter. Let the feast begin!

Notes: This is a big recipe, and Alishan usually uses two large stockpots. If you can't find dry-salted bacon, ask your butcher what they would recommend as an alternative.

Pair with: Little Farm Riesling. This is an intense, dry, racy Riesling. A beautifully aromatic wine showing apples and pears, white flowers and mandarin orange with some baking spice. The palate is crisp, intense and pure with its lemon, lime, peach, green apple and stony and chalky minerality.

Corcelettes Estate Winery

www.corceletteswine.ca

2582 Upper Bench Road, Keremeos

*O*nce upon a time, in a small town in Canada, a girl from Nunavut met a boy from Switzerland . . . The romantic story behind Corcelettes Estate Winery reads a bit like a fairy tale about destiny, and it's hard not to feel this young couple's excitement and passion for building their dream.

The stunning Keremeos vineyard estate is set on one of the Similkameen Valley's dramatic hillsides, with vineyards poetically spilling down around their home and tasting room. There is a touch of whimsy here too—they have a golf tee available for those guests who feel like whacking a ball into the hillside after their wine tasting. A special patio lounge off the tasting room is reserved for wine club members, complete with their own golf tee. As majestic as the setting is, this is also a warm family home filled with the sounds of children laughing and dogs barking.

"Our estate has such a natural beauty and charisma," says owner Jesce Baessler. "We still can't believe that what we do for a living is making great wine from an epic vineyard in the most beautiful valley we've ever seen. It's a combination of our site's natural beauty, the quality of wine we craft, our team, our family and our guests that truly makes visiting this place special." Jesce and her husband Charlie have recently expanded operations with the purchase of 132 acres right next to the current estate vineyard. It comes with a lovely five-bedroom rancher-style home that overlooks the Similkameen Valley, which they plan to turn into a wine-country B&B.

Corcelettes (KOR-sah-LETs) is named after the Baessler family farm in Switzerland, where Charlie grew up. He and his parents started Corcelettes as a micro winery in the Similkameen before expanding onto the current property. Jesce grew up in Nunavut, where she learned how to build igloos and drive dogsleds instead of playing soccer or ballet. She came to the area with her mom in 2012, when the two stumbled across Keremeos on an adventurous road trip they had planned—driving from Yellowknife to Cabo!

With a diverse agricultural background reinforced by a science degree, Charlie puts his expertise to use growing the vineyard and making the wine. "Winery and vineyard operations came naturally to Charlie," says Jesce. Their portfolio now boasts 13 wines and a growing production that currently stands at 3,500 cases—and the awards keep stacking up.

When they're not running the winery, Charlie and Jesce love watching their adorable twin girls, Arya and Evelyn, run free on their beautiful vineyard estate with the family dog, Schaze, in tow.

Nana's Roast Caribou

This recipe was a favourite dish made by Jesce's nana, Margaret Rose Laserich, for her family in the Arctic. If you don't have caribou nearby, feel free to use a regular beef pot roast to absorb the delicious flavours. And do not skip the alpine blueberry sauce! It is a treat.

Serves 6

Caribou Roast:

3–4 lb caribou, or venison or beef roast (see note)

5 cloves garlic, halved

2 Tbsp olive oil

1 tsp salt

Pepper

2 shallots or 1 onion, sliced

1 leek, sliced

3-inch piece ginger, chopped

3–4 cups good red wine

3–4 sprigs rosemary

Pinch of ground Espelette or cayenne pepper

Alpine Blueberry Sauce:

3 Tbsp butter

2 cups alpine or wild blueberries, fresh or frozen

2 Tbsp honey, or to taste

1 cup beef or vegetable stock

½ tsp ground cinnamon

Note: To ensure it cooks evenly, allow the roast to come to room temperature before you start. This should take about 2 hours. Use the time to open a nice bottle of red wine, preferably the Corcelettes Menhir, and pour yourself a glass!

For the Caribou Roast:

Preheat the oven to 300°F.

Pat the roast dry with paper towel. Using the tip of a sharp knife, make 10 small incisions around the roast and insert a garlic clove half into each incision. Rub the roast with the olive oil, sprinkle with the salt and pepper and place in a Dutch oven.

Scatter the shallots, leeks and ginger around the roast, then pour in enough red wine to come halfway up the roast. Season with the rosemary sprigs and Espelette pepper.

Cover and cook in the oven for 2½ hours, then lower the heat to 225°F for a further 30 minutes. For a smaller roast, you can shorten the cooking time by up to 1 hour.

For the Alpine Blueberry Sauce:

While the meat is roasting, in a medium-size saucepan over medium heat, melt the butter with the blueberries and honey. Bring the mixture to a simmer, then add the stock and cinnamon. Continue to simmer until the sauce reaches a thick consistency, then remove from heat.

Remove the roast from the oven, slice and serve with alpine blueberry sauce.

Pair with: Corcelettes Menhir. The Menhir of Corcelettes, Switzerland, is an iconic rock formation that stands near the castle of Grandson, from where the Baessler family originate. In this Cabernet Sauvignon and Syrah blend, look for Cabernet's stewed black fruits and Syrah's sweet and spicy pipe tobacco notes.

Vista D'oro Farms & Winery (page 195)

Fraser Valley, Vancouver Island & Gulf Islands

Fraser Valley

Vancouver Island

Gulf Islands

Introduction

Many of BC's wineries are based inland, but there are plenty of wonderful wines to be found farther west. Head towards the Pacific coast to discover the offerings of the Fraser Valley, Vancouver Island and the Gulf Islands.

The gorgeous Fraser Valley is truly an agricultural hub, with farms ranging from livestock to vegetables and everything in between. And of course, there are wineries! Although it's only an hour or so from the city of Vancouver, the Fraser Valley feels worlds away, with the beautiful, rich farmlands of Langley, Abbotsford and Chilliwack laid out like a patchwork quilt nestled in between stunning mountain ranges.

Board BC Ferries and sail over to Vancouver Island to experience the thrilling wine scene by the sea. Concentrated in the farm-rich Cowichan Bay area, the mild climate and growing conditions here have been drawing winemakers and growers to plant vineyards since 1992, when Vigneti Zanatta first opened. The excellent growing conditions (a temperate climate and the longest growing season in Canada) work for a large number of varietals, mostly white. Cowichan Bay has been recognized as an international Cittaslow destination: a place that embraces the slow-food movement, and a lifestyle that promotes craftsmanship and environmental stewardship.

The wine scene by the sea continues to grow, spreading onto the stunning Gulf Islands adjacent to Vancouver Island. The Gulf Islands are home to delightful communities, with wine and grape production on Salt Spring, Pender, Saturna, Quadra, Gabriola, Hornby and Denman. Sea Star Vineyards on Pender Island is just a ferry hop away from Victoria, and it is a sight to behold. Standing in the vineyard you are spoiled with a magical view of grapevines stretching all the way down to the sparkling ocean below.

Vista D'oro Farms & Winery

www.vistadoro.com
346–208th Street, Langley

Makers of fine preserves, organic farmers, winemakers and now food truck owners, Lee and Patrick Murphy have built a delicious agritourism destination at their home hub of Vista D'oro Farms & Winery in Langley. Their dreamy 10-acre landscape is home to dogs, cats, chickens and horses, a darling farmgate market that doubles as the tasting bar, and a big red barn that has been a venue for numerous events. The Murphys have a serious knack for hospitality and for creating amazing products.

Their farmgate shop also hosts tasting picnics outside under the old walnut tree, a special experience that offers guests a taste of Vista D'oro wine paired with locally made cheese, charcuterie and, of course, Vista D'oro's delicious preserves. The Murphys are all about community, and they work closely with other farms and wineries in the area to create the ultimate food, wine and farm experience in Langley. Another way to visit is as part of a Circle Farm Tour (which includes a stop at Vista D'oro).

It all began in a greenhouse in 2001, when the couple decided to grow produce to sell at farmers' markets. Lee then began creating delicious preserves from her orchard and garden, and decided to sell them at the wine shop. "About 80% of what is grown on the farm ends up in a jar or bottle!" explains Lee. "It began with taking my rhubarb and vanilla preserve to the farmers' markets to sell alongside our tomato plants and herbs from the farm.

The jam very quickly began outselling everything else we brought to the markets." And so, the Preservatory was born, and a sophisticated commercial kitchen was built on the farm. The preserves are now sold in fine stores across the country and abroad. In 2014 Harrods chose to retail Lee's line in their impossibly high-end food store in London. She has since published a cookbook, *The Preservatory*, and continues to create her glamorous line of seasonal preserves using traditional old-world techniques and making small batches in copper pots. She is, in fact, an official Jam Master.

Now for Patrick's story. He started making wine and growing grapes when they bought the farm, but soon decided to take the next step into commercial production. Vista D'oro gained critical acclaim in the wine world with its unique flagship walnut wine, D'oro, which has French origins. "The recipe was brought to us by our good friend Jerome," explains Patrick. "It was his great-grandfather's and dates back to 1893." From there they expanded, making a variety of estate-grown, small-batch red and white wines and apple cider.

Their newest tasty adventure is a food truck christened Pizzam! (Pizza + Jam), which serves pizzas, cheese and charcuterie boards, salad by the jar and soft-serve ice cream, all with their preserves. Yum!

You can order their products online at www.thepreservatory.com.

Lee's Croque MaJam

As a child, Lee Murphy's favourite lunch was grilled cheese and tomato soup. In this version, basic grilled cheese meets French decadence. Lee is a well-known Francophile, so this dish is the perfect expression of her passions. A croque monsieur is basically a gourmet grilled ham and cheese sandwich that is a favourite in bars, and a croque madame is the same but with the addition of a fried egg. Lee explains, "I've taken this very traditional sandwich and put it on its head—literally! The egg is under the creamy béchamel, egg-in-hole style." Très yum.

Serves 4

¼ cup unsalted butter + more for spreading

¼ cup flour

1½ cups milk, warmed

Pinch of grated nutmeg

Salt and pepper

8 slices pain du campagne, country bread or sourdough

4 Tbsp Preservatory Figs & Walnut Wine preserves

4 tsp Dijon mustard

8 slices prosciutto

1½ cups grated Gruyère cheese

4 eggs

Pepper

Pair with: D'oro. The flagship of Vista D'oro, this fortified walnut wine is a blend of Marechal Foch, Merlot, Vista D'oro's green walnuts and BC brandy. Aged for eight years in French and American oak, this artisanal fortified port-style wine is handmade in small batches from BC's finest vinifera. A truly unique offering.

In a small saucepan over medium-high heat, melt the butter. Add the flour and whisk constantly for 1–2 minutes. Add the warmed milk, whisking to combine, and heat until the mixture is bubbly and thick, about 3–5 minutes. Season with nutmeg, salt and pepper. Keep the béchamel sauce warm while assembling the sandwiches.

Preheat the oven to 375°F and line a baking sheet with parchment paper.

Remove the crusts from the bread, butter four of the slices and place them on a cutting board, buttered side down. Spread with preserves and Dijon mustard, then layer two slices of prosciutto on each and top each with ¼ cup grated cheese.

Cut an approximately 3-inch round in the remaining four slices of bread. Cover the sandwiches with the bread and discard the rounds.

Heat a frying pan over medium-high heat and add the sandwiches to the pan, buttered side down. You may need to work in batches. Cook until just browned, about 2–3 minutes, and transfer to the baking sheet.

Carefully crack an egg into each hole and season with pepper. Smother the top of each sandwich with warm béchamel and spread it to the edges with an offset spatula, taking care not to disturb the egg. Cover with the remaining Gruyère.

Bake until the sandwiches are golden brown and the egg yolk is still a bit runny, about 20 minutes. Serve with heirloom tomato soup.

Chaberton Estate Winery

www.chabertonwinery.com
1064–216th Street, Langley

Just 45 minutes from Vancouver, the landscape shifts from urban to rural, a lush, farm-rich region. Langley's best-kept secret is all the delights it offers for food and wine lovers. Chaberton Estate Winery is the Fraser Valley's oldest winery: the original owners took a leap into uncharted territory by planting vines back in 1975. The gorgeous 55-acre estate's set of winery buildings make it feel a bit like a small village. One of the highlights is the fabulous restaurant: Bacchus Bistro, with Chef Ashley Chisham at the helm, creates delicious gourmet cuisine that features local ingredients. The patio seating is a treat, with a view of the vineyard that begins just steps from where you dine.

A large operation, the winery is now producing about 60,000 cases of wine. That includes the estate-grown Bacchus, Chaberton's flagship wine, which thrives in the cooler climate of the Fraser Valley. With the exception of Gamay, the varietals are cool-weather whites similar to what one would find grown in northern France and Germany. About 20% of the grapes used in Chaberton's wine repertoire are estate-grown, with the remaining percentage grown in the Okanagan and the Similkameen Valley.

Original owners Claude and Inge Violet emigrated from France, bringing with them nine generations of viticulture and winemaking history. The Violets found their perfect terroir match on this property in the Campbell Valley, South Langley, and it became Domaine de Chaberton in 1975. The couple and the land thrived, allowing them to open a retail wine shop as a farmgate winery with a 3,000-case production in 1991—a first in the area. When the Violets retired after 25 years, they sold the business to Anthony Cheng and Eugene Kwan. One was based in Vancouver and the other in Hong Kong, but they shared a thirst for a new adventure and were both wine aficionados.

Anthony and Eugene met in 1988 through a business deal at the law firm Anthony was practising with, and they have been best friends ever since. Anthony's primary business is in commercial real estate in England, and he travels between there, Hong Kong and, now, Canada. After selling the winery, the Violets became close friends with the duo and assisted them in learning the ropes.

Pan-Roasted Fraser Valley Duck Breast with Spiced Bacchus Gastrique

This recipe was created by Executive Chef Ashley Chisham at Chaberton's eatery, Bacchus Bistro. It is a delicious celebration of the owners' Chinese roots and features duck as a tribute to Eugene Kwan's mother (it's her favourite).

Serves 2

Gastrique:

½ cup sugar

½ cup white wine vinegar

1 cup Chaberton Estate Grown Bacchus wine

1 Tbsp sliced ginger

1 Thai chili pepper, sliced

Duck:

½ Tbsp vegetable oil

1 (9 oz) Fraser Valley duck breast

Salt and pepper

3 Tbsp chicken stock

Bok Choy:

3 heads baby Shanghai bok choy

Vegetable oil

1 Tbsp toasted sesame seeds

For the Gastrique:

Place the sugar and ¼ cup of water in a small, heavy-bottomed saucepan over high heat.

Bring to a boil, then lower the heat to medium-high. Continue boiling until the syrup turns a light blond colour, about 10 minutes.

Add the vinegar and lower the heat to medium. Be careful, as the caramel is very hot and the vinegar will immediately come to a violent boil. Don't panic! Just lower the heat again and gently boil until all the caramel is dissolved.

Reduce by half, then add the Bacchus wine and reduce by half again.

Add the ginger and chilies and turn the heat to low. Allow to steep for 10 minutes, then strain through a fine strainer and discard the solids. Reserve the syrup while you prepare tshe duck breast.

For the Duck:

Preheat a heavy-bottomed sauté pan over high heat and add the vegetable oil to coat the bottom of the pan.

Season the duck with salt and pepper, then gently place it skin side down in the pan and lower the heat to medium. For a medium-rare duck breast, cook for 3–4 minutes, then lower the heat and cook for another 3–4 minutes.

Carefully flip the breast and continue to cook over low heat for another 7 minutes.

When the desired doneness is achieved, remove the breast from the pan and set aside to rest and keep warm.

Pour out the fat from the pan and deglaze with the chicken stock. Return the pan to high heat and add 5 Tbsp gastrique. Reduce by about half, or until a light syrupy consistency is achieved. Set aside for serving.

continued

For the Bok Choy:

Sauté the baby Shanghai bok choy in a little vegetable oil (or some of the rendered duck fat from the breast) until fork-tender but still slightly crisp. Toss in the sesame seeds at the end and remove from heat.

To serve, divide the bok choy between the serving plates. Slice the duck breast thinly on a slight angle, then place on top of the bok choy. Spoon the remaining gastrique over the duck, carefully coating the breast. Yum!

Pair with: Chaberton Reserve Merlot. This medium-bodied wine has a ripe blueberry and violet nose, and dried prune and raisin notes with a dark caramel/toffee on the finish. Enjoy with duck, pork, roasted vegetables, grilled mushrooms or pasta with red sauce.

Singletree Winery

www.singletreewinery.com
5782 Mt. Lehman Road, Abbotsford
1435 Naramata Road, Penticton

What fun to find a winery in the middle of the farmlands of Abbotsford! Horses and cats and dogs and turkeys and children all happily coexist on this beautiful farm that is Singletree Winery. The Etsell family live and work on this property too—their two beautiful family homes sit among manicured gardens with green grassy lawns reaching out to the lush vineyards beyond. The name Singletree comes from the name of a single-harness yoke used in the late 1800s by pioneering farmers.

This is an idyllic venue to rent for private events and weddings. Classic picnic tables under the heritage fruit trees offer a shady haven for summer visitors and a chance for city folks to unwind into the rhythm of farm life. The cute red tasting room has lots to see and buy besides wine: there are loads of gift ideas and a fridge full of local cheeses and treats, including delicious wine jellies made by owner Debbie Etsell. Everything here is tended with love.

Debbie's husband Garnet Etsell was raised on a blueberry farm in Vancouver. He chose a career in accounting, but he always dreamed of returning to the land. He spent many years working for a large agriculture business, which allowed him to keep a finger on the pulse of the industry. When a dream piece of farmland in the Mt. Lehman area became available, he and Debbie grabbed it.

Let's talk turkey. The Etsell family farm started out in the turkey-raising business, which they continue alongside the winery operation (wine and turkey are indeed an excellent pairing). Their son Andrew used to run the turkey program, but after a summer job a few years back at Mission Hill Family Estate Winery, he was drawn by the glamour of the winemaking world and presented that passion to his parents. Fully on board with this new direction, they planted vines on the property while Andrew earned his degree from University of California, Davis.

This is very much a family operation. The whole family, including Andrew's wife Laura and their two kids, live on the farm estate. The family has purchased another vineyard and winery in Naramata, offering them the opportunity to create wines from two distinct growing regions. They are currently producing 17 white wines, five reds and a rosé.

Debbie's Roasted Eggplant & Turkey Moussaka

The Etsells, the family that runs Singletree Winery, love a good comfort-food casserole, and as turkey farmers, they like to swap in this healthy alternative to red meat. Debbie roasts the eggplant instead of frying it to reduce fat and calories. The turkeys, of course, are raised locally with care.

Serves 6

Moussaka:

2–3 medium eggplants, cut into ¼-inch-thick discs

Salt, for dehydrating

5 Tbsp olive oil

1 large onion, diced

3–4 cloves garlic, minced

1 lb ground turkey

¾ cup white wine

1 cup diced fresh or canned tomatoes

5 Tbsp tomato paste

3 Tbsp ketchup

1 tsp sugar

1 tsp dried fine herbs or dried parsley

1 tsp ground cinnamon

¼ tsp ground nutmeg

½ tsp salt

Pinch of pepper

Béchamel Sauce:

1 egg

4 Tbsp butter

4 Tbsp flour

2 cups milk

½ tsp grated nutmeg

Salt and pepper

For the Moussaka:

Preheat the oven to 400°F and grease a baking sheet. Set aside.

Layer the eggplant discs onto paper towel or in a colander and sprinkle with salt. Let sit for 30 minutes to draw out the moisture and bitterness. Rinse well and pat dry with paper towel. Arrange the slices on the prepared baking sheet in one layer and drizzle with 3 Tbsp of the olive oil. Bake for 15–20 minutes, or until golden brown. Remove from the oven and set aside.

In a large frying pan over medium-high heat, sauté the onions in 2 Tbsp olive oil for about 3 minutes, then lower the heat, add the garlic and cook for about 10 minutes, or until tender. Return the heat to medium-high, add the ground turkey and cook, stirring frequently, until lightly browned. Add the wine and cook down for 2–3 minutes, then add the diced tomatoes, tomato paste, ketchup, sugar, herbs, cinnamon, nutmeg, salt and pepper. Stir to combine, cover and simmer over low heat for 25 minutes.

For the Béchamel Sauce:

In a small bowl, beat the egg and set aside.

In a medium saucepan over medium-low heat, melt the butter. Sprinkle in the flour and stir until smooth. Cook for 3 minutes, stirring constantly. Slowly add the milk, whisking to prevent lumps. Add the nutmeg, salt and pepper. Once the sauce has thickened (it should take about 2 minutes), remove from heat and very slowly add a bit of the sauce into the beaten egg. This will prevent it from cooking the egg. Add this egg mixture to the rest of the sauce and continue to whisk for another 2 minutes, then cover and let sit until assembly is complete.

Assembly:

1 cup ricotta cheese

½ cup grated Gruyère cheese

⅓ cup grated Parmesan cheese

To Assemble:

Preheat the oven to 350°F and grease a 9 × 12-inch baking dish or casserole dish.

Arrange one layer of the roasted eggplant in the dish, then spoon half the turkey mixture overtop. Cover with ricotta cheese and top with another layer of eggplant. Add the remaining turkey sauce. If you have enough roasted eggplant, place another layer down. Cover with béchamel sauce and sprinkle the Gruyère and Parmesan overtop. Bake for 50–60 minutes, or until the top is golden brown. Remove from the oven and let sit for 10 minutes before cutting into serving pieces.

Pair with: Singletree Pinot Noir. Dark brooding berry fruit intermingle with toasty, spicy French oak and forest floor with a delicious herbal note. With its silky tannins, this Pinot Noir will reward cellaring for 5–10 years.

Alderlea Vineyards

www.alderlea.ca
1751 Stamps Road, Duncan

The Cowichan Valley offers one of BC's best experiences and has become a destination for food and wine lovers. As you wind your way through the diverse geography that ranges from farm to seascape, a feeling of tranquility envelops you. This strange phenomenon is referred to as "island time," and it is why Cowichan Bay was designated an international Cittaslow town for its encouragement of the slow-food movement. You will discover Alderlea Vineyards on the rural outskirts of the small city of Duncan. It's a small but passion-fuelled operation, and Zac Brown and Julie Powell, along with their winery dog Vino, are living their dream.

After long and successful careers in health and safety (Zac) and human resources (Julie), the couple purchased the vineyard in 2017 from Roger and Nancy Dosman, who were pioneers in the Vancouver Island wine industry. Zac was born and raised on the island, so for him it was a home-coming. "We began looking at vineyards in 2009, starting on Vancouver Island and in the Okanagan," Julie explains. "While living overseas, we also seriously considered France and Italy or even further afield in New Zealand or South America."

Despite working in a different field most of his life, Zac was also a garagiste (see page 274) making his own batch of wine each year. Julie says, "We eventually decided it was time to turn our serious hobby into a new career. In 2016 we decided it was now or never to make the leap, and that we wanted to be back on Vancouver Island,

even if it meant finding a piece of land and developing it from scratch. Roger's extensive search for the right piece of land in the early '90s landed him a gently sloped, south-facing plot over Quamichan Lake, in the rain shadow of Mount Prevost. It is a near-perfect spot for growing grapes, with nutrient-rich glacial and alluvial soils." The couple is currently producing 2,000 cases of wine, but plans to increase that to 3,500 and add five acres of vines.

They are very community-minded and have plans to offer collaborative events and education workshops on-site. Their community spirit also played a role in the creation of their second label, Plaid, in addition to their Alderlea brand: "Alderlea is all estate-grown, so we created a second label, partnering with other local growers for additional grapes," Zac explains. "In July 2017 we launched the Plaid label, comprising Plaid White and Plaid Red, two easy-drinking blends." The name? "It was cold in the winery and the men on the bottling crew were all wearing plaid flannel shirts. We joked that 'real winemakers wear plaid.'"

Julie has enjoyed trading high heels for gumboots, learning to drive the tractor for harvest and working closely with Zac as business partners. "We used to joke that with all our business travel, we were married for 12 years but together for only 8. We love the location and proximity to nature. Sunrises and sunsets over the mountains are breathtaking, and we never tire of the bright and boundless stars at night."

Alderlea Wild Mushroom Soup

Alderlea Vineyards' Zac Brown says, "This is an easy recipe that, once mastered, will go a long way to establishing your reputation as a legend in the kitchen." Plain white button mushrooms from the grocery store will work just fine here, but to take this dish to the next level, use a mix. Zac typically opts for a combination of brown and white button mushrooms with a handful of dried wild mushrooms thrown in. Vancouver Island is known to food lovers for its glorious bounty of wild mushrooms, especially the coveted chanterelles that grow in the rainforests. "Make this recipe with fresh chanterelle mushrooms," Zac says, "and your guests will write songs about your kitchen prowess."

Serves 4–6

6 Tbsp butter

1 large onion, thinly sliced

2 cloves garlic, minced

4½ cups coarsely chopped mushrooms (see recipe introduction)

3 cups chicken or vegetable stock

1 cup dry white wine

1 sprig flat-leaf parsley (see note)

¼ cup sherry or port

Salt and pepper

Truffle oil or finely grated truffle, for garnish (optional)

Note: *For a bolder flavour, swap the parsley for a sprig of rosemary (this works best when using brown mushrooms, not chanterelles or white buttons).*

Melt 2 Tbsp of the butter in a saucepan over medium heat. Add the onions and garlic and sauté until soft but not browned. Add the remaining butter and the mushrooms and cook for 10 minutes, stirring occasionally.

Add the stock, wine and parsley and bring to a boil, then lower the heat and simmer, covered, for 1 hour. Pour the soup into a blender in portions and purée until smooth, or use an immersion blender to purée in the pot.

Return the blended soup to the pot (if using the blender method) and lightly simmer for 20 minutes. Add the sherry and season with salt and pepper.

Divide into bowls and serve hot. If you like, drizzle a couple of drops of truffle oil or grate a tiny amount of fresh truffle on the top of each bowl for a final flourish.

Pair with: Alderlea Bacchus. From one of Vancouver Island's oldest plantings, this is a clean, crisp white wine, with heady floral and citrus aromas and flavours of kiwi and apricot.

Vigneti Zanatta

www.zanatta.ca
5039 Marshall Road, Duncan

There is magic here. The Zanatta vineyard estate is nestled in a shire where island mountains backdrop grapevines. You will detect a hint of the sea in the air, and perhaps notes from one of the ancient fruit trees or flower gardens that dance around the yellow farmhouse/tasting room and restaurant in a peaceful portrait of a bucolic island lifestyle.

Proprietor Loretta Zanatta shares the roles of both winemaker and vineyard manager at Vigneti Zanatta with her husband Jim Moody. Loretta grew up in this enchanted farmhouse, which was once her family home and the very first estate winery on Vancouver Island. Jim grew up in the agriculture-rich valley of Pemberton, BC, and then majored in horticulture at the University of British Columbia.

Family patriarch Dionisio (Dennis) Zanatta arrived in Canada in the 1950s after leaving his home in Treviso, Italy. Loretta followed in her father's footsteps into the wine industry, and went on to study wine in Piacenza, Italy. The family officially opened up their farmgate winery in 1992 and became the first sparkling wine producer on the island. In 1996 Loretta and Jim took over the family business, with Jim becoming winemaker.

"We are proud to make uniquely Vancouver Island wine," says Loretta. With 25 acres of vines in place, the winery specializes in creating delicious sparkling wines.

Loretta took her father's winemaking to the next level after she fell in love with the art and science of the champagne method of winemaking. These days, their range includes four sparkling wines (one, Taglio Rosso, is a rare red bubbly!) packaged in lovingly hand-riddled and -disgorged bottles. All of their wines are made from grapes exclusively grown on their Glenora Vineyard.

The farmhouse is also home to the tasting room and a kitchen. Relaxing on the wide back porch with a charcuterie board and a glass of Zanatta bubbles is pure heaven.

Frittelle Venetien

Carnival Doughnuts

These little donuts are well known in the Venice area of Italy, where Loretta Zanatta's family roots lie. Frittelle are traditionally prepared for the annual Carnival extravaganza in February. Leading up to and during Carnival in Venice, you will find these bites of delight everywhere. At home, Loretta continues the tradition of making these treats the way her mother taught her for family celebrations.

Makes about 3 dozen doughnuts

½ cup raisins
½ cup rum
1½ cups flour
¼ cup sugar + more for sprinkling
1 heaping Tbsp baking powder
½ tsp salt
3 eggs
Zest of 1 orange
1 cup milk
1 tsp pure vanilla
Sunflower oil for deep-frying

Soak the raisins in the rum overnight to plump up.

In a large bowl, stir together the flour, the ¼ cup of sugar, and the baking powder and salt.

In another bowl, whisk the eggs with the orange zest; milk and vanilla.

Add the bowl of dry ingredients to the wet ingredients, stirring until the mixture is well combined and creamy.

Add the raisins and the rum they were soaking in and stir to combine. The dough should be a little thicker than pancake batter.

In a deep pan or deep fryer over medium-high heat, heat the sunflower oil to 375°F. You will need enough oil for balls of dough to sink and float in. Once the oil is hot, drop in golf ball–sized balls of batter from a teaspoon, a few at a time. Once one side is brown they will turn on their own, but you may need to keep them rolling so that they cook evenly. When golden all over, remove the balls from the oil and lay on a paper towel–lined plate to drain. Immediately sprinkle with sugar and continue cooking in batches until all are done.

Pair with: Zanatta Glenora Fantasia Brut. In 1990 Vigneti Zanatta created and released Glenora Fantasia, Vancouver Island's very first sparkling wine created in the traditional method. This utterly unique sparkling wine expresses a bouquet of green apple through an array of small, persistent bubbles.

Blue Grouse Estate Winery

www.bluegrouse.ca
2182 Lakeside Road, Duncan

Driving around the winding roads in the *Wind in the Willows*–like setting surrounding the tiny town of Duncan, you will stumble across a stunning, state-of-the-art winery. The estate's beautiful modern tasting room is surrounded by vineyards, wetland ponds and lush rainforest. Owners Paul and Cristina Brunner have created a haven here, including their second home (they also live in Lima, Peru). There is also a beautiful suite available for rent beneath their vineyard home—Grouse House is, as they call it, a "Bed & Bottle" retreat.

Paul will tell you, with his usual witty sense of humour, "After about 40 years in the mining industry, this is my penance—I've gone GREEN."

In other words, he fell in love with the estate and purchased it in 2012. Their principal home is still in Peru (Cristina has a huge family with 10 siblings there), but they wanted to have something in Canada to be close to Paul's family too. "Blue Grouse has become a gathering point for my family since I bought it, which was important to us," says Paul.

Blue Grouse has incredibly unique terroir. The warm, dry summers and mild, moist winters make the Cowichan Valley Canada's only cool maritime Mediterranean climate. The winery is fast becoming known as a producer of exceptional Pinot Noir, garnering raves and accolades by wine critics. The vineyard is certified sustainable and soon to be certified organic, and the winery came with one of the industry's most passionate winemakers, Bailey Williamson, who spent many years with the previous owner and has been able to offer Paul valuable insights into his land and the industry. The vineyard holds a wonderful place in BC wine history; it is one of the founding estate wineries on Vancouver Island.

Paul Brunner's Cured Salmon

This dish is a celebration of two cultures, where Peru meets West Coast. Blue Grouse Estate Winery's Paul Brunner says, "When I lived in Peru, I experimented with ceviche and tiradito (both well-known Peruvian dishes of raw fish marinated in lemon or lime juice) for years." The result is this delightful salmon recipe, which has become one of Paul's signature dishes.

Serves about 10 as an appetizer

1 (2 lb) skin-on fillet wild BC salmon, de-boned (see note)

1 cup sea salt

1 cup raw demerara sugar

1 Tbsp ground cinnamon

1 Tbsp black peppercorns, crushed (see note)

2 oranges, thinly sliced (see note)

1 bunch dill, chopped

2 jalapeño peppers, deveined, deseeded and sliced

1 bulb fennel, finely chopped

Chopped dill, to garnish

Chopped capers, to garnish

Notes: Make sure the salmon is sushi-grade or has been previously frozen. For the peppercorns, Szechuan or other coloured peppercorns will work as well. If you like, substitute grapefruit for the oranges.

You will need two nesting Pyrex dishes for this recipe (the larger just big enough for the fish and the curing ingredients). Line the larger dish with enough plastic wrap to wrap around the fish.

Clean the scales off the fish and give it a good wash and dry. In a bowl, thoroughly mix the salt, sugar, cinnamon and peppercorns.

Lay the fish on top of the plastic wrap in the Pyrex dish, skin side down. Place the oranges on top and add the dill, jalapeño peppers and fennel. This will separate the salt/sugar mixture from the flesh of the fish and keep it from getting too salty.

Cover thoroughly with a generous amount of the salt/sugar mixture. Pull the plastic wrap tightly around the entire fish to seal it. Place the smaller Pyrex dish on top and fill it with 8½ lb of weights (bags of rice work well).

Move the stack of dishes to the fridge and leave the salmon to cure for 48 hours. Every 12 hours, discard the liquid and flip the fish over.

After 48 hours, remove the plastic wrap and discard the seasoning ingredients, then rinse the fish well to remove any remaining salt. Pat it dry with clean paper towel. Place the fish on a baking sheet, uncovered, and return to the fridge to rest for 24 hours.

When ready to serve, slice into thin pieces with an extra-sharp knife and top with dill and capers. Serve with bagels and cream cheese, or on a platter with crostini. If you are not going to serve immediately, wrap it with plastic wrap and save in the fridge for up to 10 days.

Pair with: Blue Grouse Sparkling Paula. Named for Paul and Cristina's daughter, Paula, this sparkle starts with aromas of pear, biscuit and a bit of earthy mushroom followed by green apple and toast. Well balanced and off-dry, it finishes with elderflower and a lingering lemon-lime citrus.

Venturi-Schulze Vineyards

www.venturischulze.com
4235 Vineyard Road, Cobble Hill

This is family with a heart of green. Based on a beautiful swath of island land, the blended family of Venturi and Schulze create wines and authentic aged balsamic vinegar. The tasting room and cellar are located adjacent to the family home, making this a true farmgate winery experience. The warm welcome you get from Marilyn and Giordano will also make you feel like you are old friends and guests in their home.

The love affair between Giordano Venturi and Marilyn Schulze crossed many oceans. Giordano was born and raised in Modena (now you understand the balsamic vinegar connection), and Marilyn hails from Queensland, Australia. They met at a French language class at the University of Montreal. Vive l'amour!

Besides a love of languages, the two also share a passion for food and wine, and they decided to look at properties in the Cowichan Valley area of Vancouver Island. They bought their Cobble Hill property on the spot. Giordano had already spent 15 years with a backyard vineyard in Vancouver, and the idea of making balsamic vinegar appealed to Marilyn's science background, so this seemed like the perfect place for them to begin a new journey together.

Their gorgeous acreage is surrounded by natural forest and a deep ravine with a spring-fed creek. "The previous owners of 30 years held the same beliefs as we do," says Marilyn, "that our environment should be protected for future generations. For over 60 years at least, it has remained naturally farmed: no pesticides or herbicides."

This organic vineyard also waters itself. "We have no need for irrigation, as the roots have been encouraged to go deep," Marilyn explains. "The unique soil makeup of the terroir collects the plentiful rain in the winter and spring and keeps it accessible for the vines all year long, even during droughts."

Venturi-Schulze wines are made as naturally as possible and are a reflection of the sustainable practices that are lovingly implemented in the vineyard. They make two types of red, an array of white blends, a rosé, a sparkling and a poetic dessert wine. And then there is the vinegar. Venturi-Schulze makes real-deal balsamic vinegar, the kind that takes years to create, and the final product is worthy of Giordano's homeland region of Modena, where the best balsamic vinegar in the world is made. Giordano and Marilyn simmer their own grape juice over fire, then convert it to vinegar through the slow, natural, ancient process of aging it in barrels. They select barrels in a range of sizes and wood varieties, each of which imparts a unique character and flavour profile to the vinegar.

Marilyn's daughter Michelle and Michelle's young son Connor are involved in all areas of the business. Two other vineyard workers are Parson Russell terriers: Fang and her daughter Josie.

Michelle's Panna Cotta
with Balsamic Strawberries

This delicious dessert recipe from Michelle Schulze is the perfect way to highlight fresh Vancouver Island strawberries when they're in season and, of course, Venturi-Schulze's exclusive balsamic vinegar. This dish can easily be made ahead and makes a grand finale to any meal.

Serves 12

1 Tbsp + ¼ tsp gelatin powder

¼ cup milk

1 cup icing sugar

½ tsp salt

3 cups cream

1 tsp pure vanilla

1½ cups sour cream

1 lb ripe strawberries, sliced, or halved if small

2 tsp berry sugar

2 tsp Venturi-Schulze Classic Balsamic Vinegar

Mint sprigs, for garnish

Pair with: Venturi-Schulze Brandenburg No. 3. This sweet amber wine is named for Bach's Brandenburg Concerto no. 3. Its rich, earthy, smoky, caramel-coffee notes pair wonderfully with foie gras, charcuterie, a cheese and hazelnut platter or roasted duck.

In a small bowl, sprinkle the gelatin over the milk and set aside.

In a medium-size saucepan over medium-high heat, bring the icing sugar, salt and 2 cups of the cream to a boil, whisking occasionally.

Remove from the heat. Stir the gelatin mixture and add it to the saucepan, stirring to dissolve, then add the vanilla.

Pour the panna cotta into a large metal bowl and cool, stirring occasionally. If you need to speed up the process, cool over cold (but not iced) water.

Whisk the remaining cream to soft peaks.

Stir the sour cream so it has an even consistency, then fold it into the whipped cream. Then gently but thoroughly fold the combination into the cooled panna cotta mixture, keeping the mixture light and airy.

Pour into a single jelly mould or 12 individual ramekins (depending on how you would like to serve it) and refrigerate overnight.

To make the topping, place the strawberries in a bowl and gently stir in the berry sugar and balsamic vinegar. Leave to marinate in the fridge for 1½ hours.

To serve, unmould the panna cotta by dipping the mould or ramekins into hot water and then inverting onto a serving platter (or individual dessert plates in the case of ramekins). You may have to run a knife around the sides of the mould or ramekins and release the panna cotta on an angle over the plates.

Bring the balsamic strawberry topping to room temperature and spoon on top of the panna cotta. Garnish with mint sprigs and another drop or two of balsamic vinegar.

Unsworth Vineyards

www.unsworthvineyards.com
2915 Cameron Taggart Road #1, Mill Bay

Unsworth Vineyards has become a shining star in Vancouver Island's culinary scene and one of the top places to visit for food and wine lovers. The enchanting property features an early 1900s heritage farmhouse converted beautifully into the Unsworth Restaurant, vineyards, manicured gardens and a tasting room and wine shop.

Family-owned and -operated, Unsworth Vineyards is a passion project of Tim and Colleen Turyk after careers spanning many years in the BC fishing industry. Tim grew up on Vancouver Island and spent his summers as a boy at Shawnigan Lake, a beautiful lakeside community in the Cowichan Bay area and a favourite holiday spot for many island families. Tim's mother Marjorie spent many happy days of her childhood there as well. It was Marjorie who inspired the name for the winery: Unsworth is her maiden name.

In 1971 Tim's life path led him away from the island and northbound to a summer job at a cannery in Prince Rupert. It was there he began his career in fishing and met his wife Colleen, who was also working as a fisher. The two worked at sea for four years before entering the processing side of the company. They sold the business in 2008 and wanted a retirement project away from the fishing world.

Tim, a competing triathlete, found the Unsworth property by chance when he was out for a run. Something about the estate called to him, and it evolved into a winery project. The food and wine industry was a perfect fit, as their son Chris was pursuing his career in wine at the time. Chris has been an integral part of developing the food and farm portion of the winery.

As advocates for the local farm industry, it was natural for Tim and Colleen to find a way to support the local economy with their work. The restaurant pioneered a Community Supported Restaurant (CSR) project. CSR members prepay for off-season meals, which helps cover the business operation costs during the winter and guarantees customers for the restaurant.

The magical Cowichan Valley is blessed with the warmest average temperatures in Canada. "Although still a cool, maritime climate in terms of grapegrowing, the exceptionally long growing season allows for the flavour compounds to fully develop without concern for sugar levels—hence alcohol levels—becoming overly high," explains Tim. "This, along with the naturally fertile clay soils, allows us to create crisp, clean, flavourful, food-friendly wines."

Their wines are winning awards and changing the face of Vancouver Island's winemaking, and the family is keeping local at heart. "Our goal is to take what nature has given us and sustainably grow grapes to produce wines that are truly enjoyable to drink and that pair exceptionally well with our locally grown food," says Tim. And the winemaking? As Tim elegantly puts it, it's "the perfect collaboration of hand and land."

Pair with: Unsworth Allegro. With pronounced flavours of honey, apple and ripe peach with animated citrus and pineapple, this wine has a nice balance, medium body and a rich finish, it is a unique expression of the luscious Sauvignette and Petit Milo Vancouver Island grape varieties.

Unsworth Seafood Chowder

This delicious soup is a favourite of diners at the Unsworth Restaurant. Created by restaurant chef Maartyn Hoogeveen, it is a celebration of the Turyks' fishing history and the West Coast's beautiful bounty from the sea. Now let's make this chowdah!

Serves 6

Chowder Base:

1 small onion, diced

2 Tbsp butter

1 sprig summer savory, roughly chopped

4 cups fish stock (see note)

1 lb Yukon Gold potatoes, peeled and quartered

3 cups cream

Chowder:

3½ Tbsp canola oil

1 onion, diced in 1-inch cubes

2 carrots, diced in 1-inch cubes

3 stalks celery, diced in 1-inch cubes

1 leek, diced in 1-inch cubes

2 Yukon Gold potatoes, diced in 1-inch cubes

2 cloves garlic, minced

8 oz Vancouver Island clams, washed

8 oz Salt Spring Island mussels, washed and beards removed

8 oz fresh wild BC coho salmon, diced

8 oz fresh ling cod, diced

8 oz fresh Pacific halibut, diced

¼ cup finely chopped flat-leaf parsley

¼ cup finely chopped dill

Salt and pepper

Fresh pea shoots, to garnish (optional)

Edible flowers, to garnish (optional)

Focaccia, to serve

For the Chowder Base:

Place the onions and butter in a large pot over medium heat. Add the savory and sweat for 4–5 minutes, taking care not to brown the onions.

Add the fish stock and potatoes and bring to a boil, then turn down to a simmer until the potatoes are fully cooked, about 20 minutes.

Cool and transfer to a blender (be careful of splashing) or use an immersion blender to blitz until smooth.

Return the chowder to the pot over low heat, and stir in the cream.

For the Chowder:

In a large frying pan over medium heat, heat the oil, then add the onions, carrots, celery, leeks, potatoes and garlic. Sauté for about 5 minutes, making sure the vegetables do not begin to brown.

Add the cooked vegetables to the chowder base and stir. Turn up the heat to medium and let simmer until just tender, about 10–15 minutes.

Add the clams, mussels and fish and bring back to a boil. Simmer until the mussels and clams open, about 4–5 minutes, then turn off the heat. Discard any of the clams or mussels that did not open. Pick out the meat from the clams and mussels, return to the chowder and discard the shells.

Stir in the parsley and dill and season to taste. Divide between bowls, top with pea shoots and edible flowers if you like, and serve with fresh focaccia.

The chowder base (without the vegetables and fish) freezes well. Thaw it in the fridge for 24 hours before use—if you try heating it up from frozen, it will just burn on the bottom of the pan.

Note: If you can't find fish stock, you can substitute vegetable stock or a mix of chicken stock and clam juice.

Sea Star Vineyards

www.seastarvineyards.ca
6621 Harbour Hill Drive, Pender Island

S ea Star Vineyards' wine labels alone will have you hearing a call to the ocean. Featuring nature's beautiful art of the sea star, the labels make the perfect introduction to the winery and vineyard on exquisite Pender Island. Seeing the vines rolling down to meet the ocean is pure poetry.

Just a quick ferry ride from Victoria or Vancouver, Pender Island is one of BC's Southern Gulf Islands. The winery has been a glorious addition to the small community of full-time islanders, and owner David Goudge and husband/winery partner Mark Anderson's warmth and unstoppable enthusiasm have helped put Sea Star on the island's must-visit list. They host farmers' markets and long-table dinners on-site and have other exciting event plans in the works.

David discovered Pender Island on a trip to Poets Cove with his mother and fell instantly in love with the island's beauty and culture. He and Mark eventually held their wedding reception at Poets Cove. David is the face and voice behind the marketing of the wine, with Mark on-site as general manager at the winery. Together they have built a brand that is making a huge splash on the wine scene.

The couple has now acquired a vineyard just across the water on the neighbouring island of Saturna as well. When standing in the vineyard at Sea Star, you can actually look across the sparkling sea and spot the vines on their new property. Plans are in the works to create sparkling wines from the Saturna property.

The winemaker at Sea Star is Ian Baker, whose out-of-the-gate award-winning wines have quickly grown a cult following. They sell out fast, with sommeliers and fans banging on the door for more.

On the unique terroir, David explains, "Pender and Saturna both enjoy long warm summers but are not exceedingly hot, so we don't need to irrigate our vineyards. This results in smaller grapes and a lower yield, but they pack a punch. Both vineyards have a slope to the ocean, which works in the winery's favour: the evening breeze helps prevent mildew, and Pender's rocky terraces and Saturna's cliffs backing the vineyards both generate heat that benefit the grapes."

Sea Star Salmon Wellington

Sea Star Vineyards' Mark Anderson has created this quick and easy version of the classic dish, and it will make you look like a culinary star. He and husband David Goudge like to serve it at dinner parties at the winery. It's also fantastic served cold as part of a picnic spread (see page 263).

Serves 4–6

1 cup mayonnaise

½ cup Dijon mustard

1 leek (white and light green parts only), cleaned and thinly sliced

1 Tbsp chopped basil

1 Tbsp chopped dill

1 tsp chopped thyme

½ tsp garlic powder

4 (each 6 oz) skinless fillets wild BC sockeye salmon

Salt and pepper

1 package frozen puff pastry (2 sheets), thawed

½ cup feta cheese, crumbled

1 cup packed baby spinach leaves, chopped

1 egg, beaten, for brushing

Preheat the oven to 375°F.

In a bowl, mix together the mayonnaise, mustard, leeks, basil, dill, thyme and garlic powder.

Season the salmon with salt and pepper and set aside. Line a baking sheet with parchment paper.

Gently roll out the puff pastry sheets into large rectangles. Cut the pastry into four individual pieces large enough to wrap around each fillet with enough overlap to seal the seams.

Place one salmon fillet in the middle of each rectangle of pastry, with the greyish-hued skinned side facing up (this way, when you flip and bake it, the greyish hue will not be noticeable on the bottom). On top of each piece, spread a quarter of the mayonnaise, mustard and herb mixture; then sprinkle with a quarter of the crumbled feta cheese and ¼ cup of the chopped spinach.

Fold the sides of the pastry into the middle to just overlap and seal. Then fold the ends in to complete the bundle. Make sure the ends are not too thick when folded (remember, the pastry puffs up!), and trim if necessary. Pinch to make sure the package is sealed. Place on the prepared sheet, seam side down.

With a sharp knife, cut a cross-hatch pattern of slits into the pastry and brush the tops with the beaten egg. Bake until the pastry is golden brown, about 45 minutes. Serve with a simple salad of fresh local greens tossed with a light lemony vinaigrette.

Pair with: Sea Star Vineyards Blanc de Noir. This pretty Pinot Noir rosé offers hints of strawberry, cranberry and rhubarb. It pairs beautifully with seafood, poultry and spicier food choices, as well as salads and lighter summer fare.

Fort Berens Estate Winery (page 241)

Lillooet, Thompson Valley, Shuswap & Kootenays

Lillooet

Thompson Valley

Shuswap

Kootenays

Introduction

While the majority of BC's wineries are concentrated in the regions covered in the previous chapters, there are plenty of great winery experiences to be had in a variety of spots around the province. Lillooet, the Thompson Valley, Shuswap and the Kootenays are all relatively new wine regions, each offering spectacular landscapes and terroir. The "Great White North" of the BC wine world offers wine lovers an incredible opportunity to taste lesser-known cool-climate varietals like Ortega, Siegerrebe or Madeleine Angevine—wines that are well known in Europe, but not yet here.

One of the oldest towns in BC, Lillooet offers beautiful rugged sights and scenery. The climate here is surprisingly similar to the Okanagan Valley's, offering long, hot, dry summers and four distinct seasons. There is only one wine destination here so far, Fort Berens Estate Winery, and it is worth the trek. An alpine setting with a dramatic backdrop of mountains, Lillooet was a base for prospectors during the gold rush and has plenty of stories and history lessons to share.

Heading east to the Thompson Valley and Kamloops, you will find another new wine region, recently announced as its own BC appellation. The semi-arid conditions and range of microclimates provide many different grapegrowing opportunities. The great Thompson River runs through the valley, feeding the farms and vineyards. The scenery ranges from sage grasslands and mountains to ranches and farms, all reminiscent of the Wild West.

The Shuswap wine region is the coolest of BC's interior wine regions and one of the most northerly grapegrowing regions in North America. Shuswap Lake is the hub, surrounded by lush cedar forests and hills that offer a year-round playground for outdoor enthusiasts. Breweries, farms and farmers' markets abound, and there are self-guided tour maps to help take it all in. The local Indigenous peoples have a rich history here and offer wonderful immersive experiences like guided interpretive tours or even the chance to participate in a powwow.

The Kootenays, the newest emerging wine region and closest to the Alberta border, now have five wineries to boast about. The area has always been renowned for the rugged beauty of the Rocky Mountains and is now also creating a buzz in the wine world, garnering excellent reviews.

Fort Berens Estate Winery

www.fortberens.ca
1881 Highway 99 North, Lillooet

Lillooet is located on the Fraser River two hours southwest of Kamloops, and man, does this little town have stories to tell! During the gold rush days in the 1860s, Lillooet was the largest North American centre west of Chicago and north of San Francisco. Prospectors struck gold in Lillooet in the 1830s; they tried to keep it a secret, but word got out. Gold fever set in, and 10,000–15,000 people travelled by boat through Victoria and onward to Lillooet. A much quieter town now, its newest claim to fame is the Fort Berens Estate Winery, the only winery in the area. Set against a dramatic mountainscape, the spectacular glass-walled winery is a popular venue for events, and the outdoor patio is home to a seasonal restaurant.

Founding partners Heleen Pannekoek and Rolf de Bruin came to BC from the Netherlands in 2005 with a dream of starting a winery. They did their research and discovered that the climate and soil conditions in Lillooet are similar to those of the South Okanagan: retreating glaciers have left gravelly soil with a thin loamy, sandy cap, which results in excellent drainage and great conditions for vines. They decided to become pioneers in this budding wine region and moved with their two young children from Europe in 2009. The couple welcomed partners to the business to allow them to expand into a 65-acre estate with Riesling, Pinot Gris, Chardonnay, Pinot Noir, Cabernet Franc and Merlot.

Most Fort Berens wine labels feature horses, but not their 23 Camels. Rolf tells the story of John Galbraith, a prospector in town back in 1862, who decided that camels would be better suited for working in Lillooet's hot, dry climate than horses: "He went down to San Francisco, where apparently camels were for sale, and bought 24 camels (one died en route). John employed the camels as a pack train and learned many things. It was true that the camels were able to pack quite a load. They were also very comfortable with the hot, dry climate. What was more difficult was that the wagon trail was quite narrow in places, and when his camel train encountered a horse train, passing each other was quite tense. The camels did not like the horses; the horses did not like the camels. This did not make John a very popular guy in town. At some point, John decided to let the camels roam, and sightings of camels were reported as late as 1908, when a First Nations chief was photographed on a camel."

Pair with: Fort Berens Late Harvest Riesling. This expressive Late Harvest Riesling bursts with notes of honey, mango and warm, caramelized bananas.

Dutch Hangop

Creamy Yogurt Dessert

Traditionally, this recipe is made with Belle de Boskoop apples (known in Dutch as Schone van Boskoop or Goudreinette). The cultivar was first identified in the 1850s by an orchardist in Boskoop, a small agricultural town in the heart of the Netherlands, roughly equidistant from Amsterdam, The Hague and Utrecht. All the elements in this recipe can be made ahead and assembled just before serving.

Serves 4

Yogurt:

4 cups plain yogurt (do not use Greek as it is already thickened)

1 Tbsp sugar

1 cup cream

Apples:

½ Tbsp unsalted butter

1 lb Belle de Boskoop apples, unpeeled, cut into ½-inch pieces (see note)

1 Tbsp brown sugar

1 tsp ground cinnamon or Dutch speculaas spices (see note)

Crumble Topping:

1½ cups flour

1 cup berry sugar

½ cup rolled oats

1 tsp ground cinnamon or Dutch speculaas spices

1 cup unsalted butter, melted

For the Yogurt:

Place the yogurt in a strainer lined with a linen cloth and set above a bowl. Cover with a lid and put in a cool spot (or the fridge) for at least 12 hours. After straining, scoop the yogurt out of the cloth and put it in another container until you're ready to use it.

Mix the sugar into the cream and whip until stiff peaks form. Just before using the yogurt, fold in the whipped cream.

For the Apples:

In a large frying pan over medium heat, melt the butter. Add the apples and sauté slowly until they start to soften. Add the brown sugar and cinnamon and sauté a few minutes longer, until the sugar is melted and sticky. Remove from heat and reserve for serving.

For the Crumble Topping:

Preheat the oven to 350°F. Mix the flour, sugar, oats and cinnamon with the butter in a bowl until roughly blended. Spread out on a baking sheet and bake for 15 minutes, or until golden brown. Cool the crumble on the sheet and set aside until ready to use.

To Serve:

Divide the yogurt into bowls. Top with warm apples and finish with crumble topping. Enjoy!

Notes: Belle de Boskoop apples are generally firm, tart and fragrant, with a high acid content that makes them great for cooking. In Lillooet, Belle de Boskoop apples are grown in an organic orchard at Bruin's End Orchard, run by long-term residents Trevor and Sarah Chandler. If you can't find Belle de Boskoop apples in your area, feel free to substitute Gala apples instead. Speculaas spices are a traditional blend of spices best known for use in the Dutch windmill cookies.

Sagewood Winery

www.sagewoodwinery.ca
589 Meadow Lark Road, Kamloops

Sagewood Winery was the very first estate winery in Kamloops and is home to the area's oldest commercial vines. Located in a rural neighbourhood above Monte Creek, this micro winery makes super-small-lot wines in a converted garage tasting room and winery. Visiting Sagewood Winery is like visiting Doug and Shelley Thompson's home, and the welcome you will receive will warm your heart.

Doug is a semi-retired family physician. "In fact, he still juggles being a family doctor along with all of his responsibilities and roles here at Sagewood," says Shelley. She is also busy as a full-time elementary school teacher, and they have two children, Nik and Emmarie. The winery plan was in motion for a very long time before it manifested and they found the ideal property to plant the vineyard. Doug is a diehard farmer at heart and loves growing things. In addition to the grapevines, there are large vegetable gardens on the property, and each of the kids has their own—Doug taught them to grow their plants from seed.

Doug brought this vineyard to life. Shelley says, "Doug has propagated 90% (if not more) of the grapes in our vineyard from clippings that were given to him by various vineyards in the Okanagan. He has hand-planted every single vine in our vineyard, and he is the only one who hand-tends to each and every vine."

This winery is a real labour of love, with no paid staff. Doug is the propagator, planter, pruner, vineyard manager, winemaker and tasting room staff—and all of his wines are handcrafted.

Sagewood is a member of the garagiste community in BC (see page 274), a group of small-lot (under 2,000 cases) wine producers who participate in an annual tasting festival (www.garagistenorth.com). Sagewood Winery is currently producing about 600 cases of wine and will keep it that way, with no plans to increase production or purchase grapes. Shelley adds with her big smile, "What I love most about the wine business is the family time and the shared experiences that it allows us as a family-owned and -operated business. Our kids are on this journey with us in every aspect possible. I love the farm-to-table lifestyle that we have been given. And I absolutely love sharing our wines and our passion with our guests in our boutique and intimate tasting room."

I guess you could say, the wine doctor is in.

Shelley's Roasted Squash Soup

Sagewood Winery's Thompson family loves eating squash from their garden, and this smooth and creamy soup combines three of their favourite types—acorn, butternut and spaghetti squash. Shelley has also tried substituting other "meaty"-textured squash varieties with great success. Serve with homemade buns for a wonderful comfort meal on a cool day.

Serves 6

1 small butternut squash, halved

1 acorn squash, halved

½ spaghetti squash (cut lengthwise)

3 Tbsp butter or olive oil

1 large onion, chopped

3 cloves garlic, minced

1 Tbsp minced ginger

1 tsp curry powder

2 Granny Smith or other tart apples, peeled and cut into ½-inch cubes

⅔ cup sherry

5 cups water or vegetable stock

1 tsp salt

Pepper

Pinch of cayenne (optional)

Preheat the oven to 400°F.

Lay the squash halves cut side down on baking sheets and roast them until the flesh is soft, about 45 minutes (the spaghetti squash may take a bit longer). When the squashes have cooled a little, scoop out the seeds and discard them, then scoop the flesh of the squashes into a large bowl.

Heat the butter in a medium saucepan over medium heat. Add the onions and sauté, stirring frequently, until softened, about 5 minutes. Add the garlic, ginger and curry powder, and cook, stirring, for 1 minute. Add the apples and the sherry, and simmer until the apples soften, about 10 minutes.

In a blender or food processor, purée the squash flesh with the water in batches. Transfer the squash purée to a large saucepan, then purée the apple-sherry mixture and add this to the puréed squash.

Heat the soup and season it with the salt, pepper to taste and, if you like, cayenne. Ladle the hot soup into bowls and serve.

Pair with: Sagewood Siegerrebe. With bouquets of lychee and melon on the nose, this high-altitude varietal offers a tropical palate with lychee overtones.

Sunnybrae Vineyards & Winery

www.sunnybraewinery.com
3849 Sunnybrae Canoe Point Road, Tappen

Sunnybrae Vineyards & Winery is a family-run business with a great sense of humour. The first clue is the name of their flagship red wine blend, Redneck Red, and the second, a boxed wine named Happy Camper. How could you not instantly love this small-town winery?

In addition to the good humour and warm family ambiance here, there are extraordinary views of Bastion Mountain, Shuswap Lake and Mount Ida. Sunnybrae is also the only winery in BC that can be accessed by boat! Visitors are welcome to tie up at the dock and stroll up to the tasting room—a fun option for summer boaters.

The winery is located in the town of Tappen, a rural community 20 kilometres (12 miles) from the city of Salmon Arm. Tappen has its own unique microclimate perfect for growing grapes and is also home to Recline Ridge Vineyards & Winery. The town's year-round residents are families who have lived there for generations. In the summer, the population swells when the community of seasonal homeowners return to the shores of Shuswap Lake.

Each year, fun-loving visitors migrate to the area on a quest for the great outdoors. It was these people who inspired the winery's fun themes. "We have a big draw of campers each summer, with people coming from all over the world to visit Shuswap Lake," says Kristie (Turner) Smolne, co-owner and manager. "With a provincial campground just down the road, it eventually struck us that these are the customers that we should be paying tribute to!"

Sunnybrae Vineyards & Winery has over 100 years of farming history to celebrate, and the tasting room walls feature a gallery of photos of the five generations of Turners who have farmed this land, as well as a display of interesting vintage artifacts. Their ancestor Charles Mobley moved to the Sunnybrae area in 1905, and his descendants farmed hay and raised cattle for many years before the land became a vineyard. The vineyard was planted in 2005 when Barry Turner retired from his business, HTK Roadbuilders (sweetly named for his three daughters, Heidi, Terry and Kristie), to spend more time with his family. He and his wife Nancy, with their whole family involved, planted the 7.5 acre vineyard with cool-climate vines, including four whites of German origin (Siegerrebe, Ortega, Kerner and Schönburger) and one of French origin (Marechal Foch). Sadly, Barry passed away in 2017, but his legacy continues through the spirit of the winery and his loving family.

Sunnybrae's Mulled Wine

Sunnybrae Vineyards & Winery hosts an annual Christmas open house, and the family's aromatic mulled wine recipe is always a hit. This local favourite is the perfect antidote for a cold winter's day and is sure to get you into the holiday spirit. It will also make your home smell like a Christmas dream.

Serves 12–15

2 clementines or 1 orange

1 lemon

1 lime

1 cup sugar

8 whole cloves

1 stick cinnamon

½ tsp grated nutmeg

⅓ vanilla bean, halved lengthwise, or ½ tsp pure vanilla

2 bottles red wine (preferably from Sunnybrae)

2 pods star anise

Remove the peels of the citrus fruits in large pieces (leaving the thick white pith on the fruit) and reserve, then juice the fruits. In a large saucepan, combine the citrus peels and juices, sugar, cloves, cinnamon stick, nutmeg and vanilla. Pour in just enough wine to cover, and bring the mixture to a simmer over medium-high heat.

Let the mixture simmer, stirring, until the sugar has completely dissolved into the wine, then increase the heat and bring to a rolling boil. Boil until the mixture becomes a thick syrup, about 4–5 minutes, then turn the heat to low.

Add the star anise and the rest of the wine. Heat gently until warm, about 5 minutes, letting all the ingredients sink to the bottom. Do not boil, as you will lose the alcohol (heaven forbid!).

Ladle into glasses, garnish as you like and enjoy. Fa-la-la-la-la, la-la-la-la!

Pair with: The holiday spirit!

Larch Hills Winery

www.larchhillswinery.com
110 Timms Road, Salmon Arm

When you are in the Shuswap region, follow the rural forest-lined road all the way to the top of Timms Road in Salmon Arm and you will find yourself atop one of the Larch Hills, with an astonishing view of the Shuswap. The Larch Hills area is a destination for outdoor enthusiasts. There are hiking and biking trails galore, and the area has become a haven for cold-weather sports fanatics, with snowmobiling, ice fishing and a world-renowned cross-country ski trails system. And then, there is wine.

Touted as the highest-altitude winery in BC at 2,300 feet (700 metres), Larch Hills Winery is also a pioneer grapegrower in this newer BC wine region. The land was all deep forest in 1987, when Hans and Hazel Nevrkla began the arduous task of converting the estate to a vineyard. Nobody had grown European varietal wine grapes so far north before. In 1990 the first Ortega variety vines were planted, and local history made. In 1997 Larch Hills Winery officially opened, joining the ranks of the province's earliest winemakers.

The Nevrklas were very supportive to new growers in the area and offered their services as consultants to burgeoning wineries. They also stayed on to consult with Jack Manser when he purchased Larch Hills Winery in 2005. Jack moved to Canada from Switzerland in 1992 and settled into the life of a dairy farmer in Millet, Alberta. The hills of the Shuswap captured his imagination, and with his history as a forester in his homeland, he felt a connection to this alpine property.

Jack's son Roman moved here to join the family business, and is managing winery operations, learning every part of the business firsthand from his dad. He and his wife Sasha are hosting plenty of events at the winery, running a wine club and planning for a bistro in the future.

Jack's great success in cool-climate wines has attracted a loyal customer base and plenty of attention from wine aficionados and media. High-altitude vineyards mean zesty cool-climate varietals, including Ortega, Siegerrebe, Madeleine Angevine and Semillon—all common in the European market regions, but harder to find in BC wine country (until now!).

Manser Family's Cheese Fondue

It's true: the Swiss love a fondue! Traditional cheese fondues are perfect for parties and cozy winter nights—they are really more of a social event than a meal. Fondue also pairs perfectly with wine.

Serves 6–8

1 clove garlic, halved

12 oz Gruyère cheese, grated

8 oz Emmenthal cheese, grated

4 oz Appenzeller or Vacherin cheese, grated

1 Tbsp + 1 tsp cornstarch

1 cup dry white wine (preferably Larch Hills Semillon)

1 tsp lemon juice

1½ Tbsp Kirsch liqueur

Pinch of white pepper, freshly ground

Pinch of grated nutmeg

1 loaf (or more) good bread or French baguette, cubed

Rub the inside of a cheese fondue pot with the garlic clove, then discard the garlic.

In a bowl, toss the grated cheeses with the cornstarch.

Place the wine and lemon juice in the fondue pot, heat until starting to simmer, then mix in the cheeses a little at a time until melted and gooey, about 5 minutes on low heat.

Add the Kirsch and a generous pinch each of pepper and nutmeg to taste. Cook, stirring gently, until creamy and smooth, about 5–7 minutes. If the fondue is too thin, mix a sprinkle of cornstarch with a splash of white wine and stir it in. If it's too thick, add a splash more wine. If it curdles or breaks, bring to a boil and whisk with a dash of lemon juice to smooth it out.

Serve with lots of bread and wine. You can also enjoy fondue with steamed red potatoes, slices of pear or vegetables like steamed broccoli and cauliflower.

Pair with: Larch Hills Pinot Gris. Discover a hint of lemon and pear in this well-balanced French varietal. It pairs well with creamy cheese fondue, chicken, fish or mussels.

Wynnwood Cellars

www.wynnwoodcellars.com
5566 Highway 3A, Wynndel

Look out, wine world, there is a new region taking root on the scene. With five wineries and counting, the glorious Kootenays region of BC is becoming its own micro food and wine destination.

The Kootenays is a beacon for outdoor enthusiasts. Not only is it home to four of the province's seven national parks, it also encompasses four mountain ranges—the Rockies, Purcells, Selkirks and Monashees—making the area ideal for backcountry adventures like skiing, mountain biking or hiking.

The Creston area has been a fruit-growing area for a long time, so the soil has proven viable.

Wynnwood Cellars is located in tiny Wynndel, just outside of Creston, and is owned by local Michael Wigen and Dave Basaraba, a grower and winemaker who moved from Walla Walla in search of new wine territories in 1987.

Burgundian varieties are thriving here, and Wynnwood's Pinot Noir and Chardonnay are proving themselves winners. "This region is defined by great sun in growing season, moderate temperatures and great minerality," explains winemaker Dave Basaraba. "We are in the Upper Columbia Basin and our winter lows are moderated by the Pacific. The entire Pacific Northwest gets tremendous sun from June to October. Our higher elevation (1,800 feet) allows for cool nights, and our minerality is comparable to northern Italy near the Dolomites. This combination results in small fruit with thick skin."

The Wigen name is famous in these parts; Michael's great-grandfather O.J. Wigen was a pioneer to the region, arriving around 1887. He and Michael's grandfather Monrad extended the family farming business by building a mill and then expanding it into a small box factory, the Wynndel Box and Lumber Co., incorporated in 1913. Michael, too, is branching out—this time, by entering the wine industry.

Michael shares a little family history: "The last boxes were produced in the early 1970s. The mill's nickname was 'Wynnwood,' so that was the logical choice for our vineyard and winery biz."

Grandma Bud's Raisin Cookies

Michael Wigen's grandma, Rosebud Wigen, was nicknamed "Bud." These cookies were a favourite of her four children, Jack, Bob, Donna and Dick, and then of her many grandchildren. These are wonderfully old-fashioned cookies that are sure to drum up happy memories. Try to eat just one . . .

Makes about 2 dozen cookies

1 cup raisins
2 cups flour
½ tsp baking powder
½ tsp baking soda
½ tsp salt
½ tsp ground cinnamon
½ tsp ground cloves
½ tsp allspice
½ cup butter, room temperature
2 small eggs, beaten
¾ cup sugar
½ cup chopped walnuts

Preheat the oven to 400°F. Line a baking sheet with parchment paper.

In a small saucepan, bring ½ cup of water to a boil. Add the raisins and cook until they plump up, about 2 minutes. Set aside to cool.

In a bowl, sift together the flour, baking powder, baking soda, salt and all the spices, and set aside.

In the bowl of a stand mixer fitted with the paddle attachment, cream the butter on medium speed for 1 minute. Turn the speed to low and add the eggs and sugar. Slowly add the flour combination, mixing until well combined. Stir in the raisins and walnuts.

Using two spoons or a small ice-cream scoop, drop balls of the dough onto the prepared baking sheet. Press down on each cookie with a fork to make them a uniform size. Bake until just turning golden brown, about 10–12 minutes. Move to a cooling rack.

Pair with: Wynnwood "Rosebud" Merlot. This dark, weighty wine was named for Grandma Bud, and shows with overtones of blackberry with hints of mint and black pepper. Undertones are of smoky tobacco and a touch of chocolate. It pairs best with pastas and your finest cuts of beef (or her cookies!).

Seasonal Menus

Spring & Summer

Bubbles & Brunch Buffet

Sunday morning fun with friends around the table is a perfect excuse
to pop the cork and make mimosas! Pair with the bubbly of your choice.

Lee's Croque MaJam, page 197

Zwiebelkuchen (Onion Quiche), page 81

Annabel's Greek Orange & Almond Cake, page 37
Fresh Okanagan fruit of your choice

Bud Break Bash: Spring-a-Ling!

That moment in April when the grapevine buds swell and pop definitely
calls for a celebration dinner! Pair with the Viognier of your choice.

Paul Brunner's Cured Salmon, page 219

Silkscarf's Upside-Down Grape-Leaf Rice, page 76
Florence's Tarragon Chicken, page 159
Grilled asparagus

Lucy Mary's Lemon Meringue Pie, page 57

Midsummer Night Magic

What could be finer than a table in the garden laden with food and wine, when the day
has cooled slightly but is still deliciously warm? Pair with the rosé of your choice.

Mamie's Scallops "à la Flamande," page 147

———✦———

Seared Arctic Char with Parsley Crust, page 167
Janice's Chicken Marbella, page 117
Sliced heirloom tomatoes with basil

———✦———

Jennifer's Pinotage Rosé Wine Jelly, page 41

Picnic on the Beach

Pack your picnic blanket and a basket filled with these make-ahead goodies, then head to
the seaside to enjoy your feast . . . don't forget the wine! Pair with the Pinot Noir of your choice.

Federico's Shrimp Ceviche, page 15
German Potato Salad, page 123

———✦———

Sea Star Salmon Wellington, page 231
Fresh greens with edible flowers and a light honey vinaigrette

———✦———

Michelle's Panna Cotta with
Balsamic Strawberries, page 223

Fall & Winter

Harvest Celebration

BC wineries are buzzing with activity as they race against the clock to pick the grapes at their peak. Pair with the Pinot Noir of your choice.

Alderlea Wild Mushroom Soup, page 211

※———————※

Chicken Cacciatore with Semolina Polenta, page 101

Diana's Fried Green Tomatoes, page 135

※———————※

Rose's Hubbard Squash Chiffon Pie, page 97

Crush Party Lunch Break

Now we have modern machinery that does the trick, but some Okanagan wineries have events where you can roll up those pant legs and stomp to your heart's content. Pair with the Chardonnay of your choice.

Shelley's Roasted Squash Soup, page 243

※———————※

Nonna's Panino, page 109

Vegetable crudités

※———————※

Coronation Grape Streusel Coffee Cake, page 45

Après-Ski Dinner

This hearty meal is sure to recharge the spirit and put you in the mood
for après-ski festivities. Pair with the bubbly of your choice.

Charlie's Äelplermagronen (Alpine Mac & Cheese), page 105
Sautéed kale

Frittelle Venetien (Carnival Doughnuts), page 215
Sunnybrae's Mulled Wine, page 247

Cozy Winter's Night Feast

Long cozy nights by the fireside are best paired with delicious BC wine
and rich feasts. Pair with the red blend of your choice.

Manser Family's Cheese Fondue, page 251

Coulombe Family Tourtière, page 150
Roasted root vegetables

Dutch Hangop (Creamy Yogurt Dessert), page 239

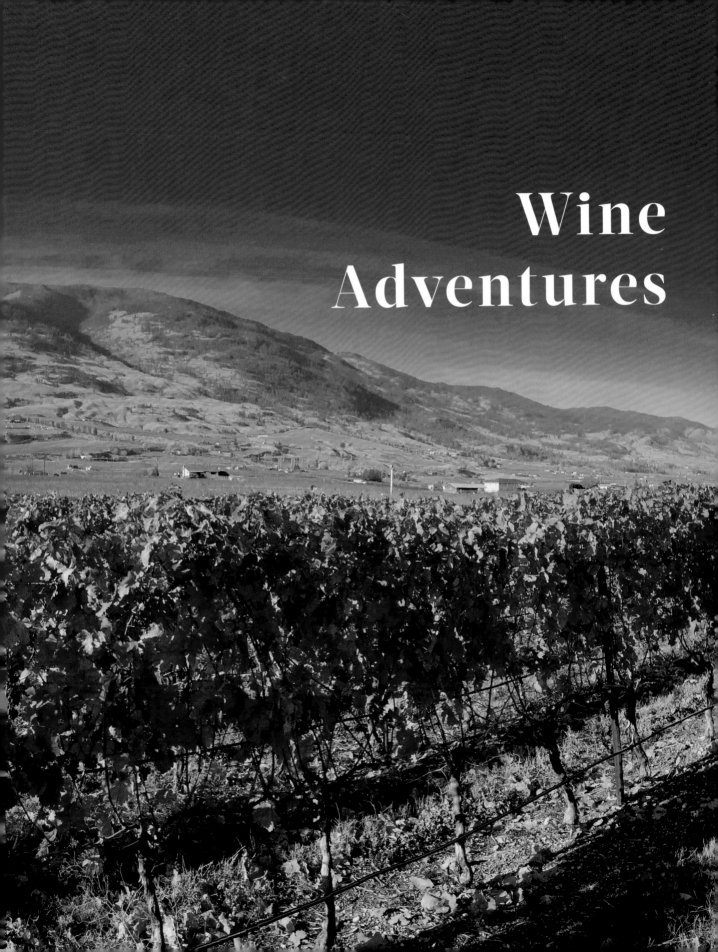

Wine
Adventures

The Great White (& Red) North

North of Vernon, from Shuswap to Kamloops and on to Lillooet, there are some enticing wine experiences to be had. These stops may be slightly off the main wine path, but they're definitely worth the trip. Many of these wineries feature cool-climate wines like Ortega, Siegerrebe and Madeleine Angevine.

For this Weekend Adventure you can either fly into Kelowna or Kamloops, or drive. If you don't mind the extra driving, base yourself at the Quaaout Lodge in Chase for an amazing experience. Owned and operated by the Little Shuswap Lake Indian Band of the Secwepemc First Nation, the lodge offers the opportunity to learn about their history and culture. Otherwise, Kamloops is a good bet to set up camp, especially if you are flying in. Better yet, add a day and make this a long weekender.

Day One

Head to Salmon Arm for an adventure on top of the world at **Larch Hills Winery** (page 249). The highest-altitude winery in the country, it offers soaring views and an oh-so-charming Swiss alpine–styled tasting room. Try their entire lineup of cool-climate whites, as well as some interesting reds like the Lemberger.

En route to **Sunnybrae Vineyards & Winery** (page 245) in Tappen, you will travel along the gorgeous Shuswap Lake, so plan ahead to stop in Salmon Arm at **DeMille's Farm Market** to pick up some local picnic treats. Enjoy your picnic on the shores of the lake or among the cedar forests. At Sunnybrae, the Redneck Red blend is delicious, and you will want to grab a few bottles to go.

Make a reservation for dinner at **Jack Sam's Restaurant at Quaaout Lodge**—they serve a fabulous Indigenous-inspired menu.

Day Two

Time for a 2½-hour journey to Lillooet. **Fort Berens Estate Winery** (page 237) is the start of the Gold Rush Trail, and backdropped by a stunning majestic mountainscape. They are the only winery in the area, and they are making spectacular wines. You can stay for lunch here and enjoy the entire experience. The Cabernet Franc is a must, but plan to taste through their entire portfolio.

Backtrack to Kamloops to visit the tiny garagiste-style **Sagewood Winery** (page 241) at the home of owners Shelley and Doug Thompson. Taste their lineup of wines, including the popular Siegerrebe (ask Doug about the wasps).

If you have time for another stop, or plan to add another day, there are a few other wineries to choose from in Kamloops, including **Privato Vineyard & Winery** and **Monte Creek Ranch Winery**.

Get Your Sparkle On!

Victory, celebration and romance are all best with bubbles, especially in the Okanagan. Whether or not you have a specific event to celebrate, put on your party hat and let's toast BC sparkling wine!

Base yourself in Kelowna at the **Hotel Eldorado** or in West Kelowna at the **Cove Lakeside Resort**. If you are arriving by plane, land at the Kelowna airport.

Day One

After breakfast, wind your way to Naramata. Destination: **Bella Wines** (page 111). Jay Drysdale is making history at his boutique sparkling wine house—and yes, he makes only bubbles.

If you have time, **Blue Mountain Vineyard & Cellars** in Okanagan Falls is another destination bubble house and a sparkling wine pioneer in BC.

Next, POP over to **Fitzpatrick Family Vineyards** (page 71) for a little sparkle by the lake. Located on beautiful Greata Ranch just outside of Summerland, this is a great spot for a tasting and then lunch at the lakeview restaurant.

Bubble on over to **Indigenous World Winery** (page 47) in West Kelowna for a taste of their sparkling rosé beauty: La'p Cheet. You may want to call in advance to check availability, as they have a limited supply. Book dinner at your accommodations—both the Eldorado and the Cove have great local wine lists.

Day Two

Cross the lake and head up to **The View Winery & Vineyard** (page 39) in Kelowna. This awesome tasting room (featuring the sexy red shoe) is a wonderful mix of glamour and farm history, and they have delicious sparkling wines to taste. Some come in bottles, and some in cans (really!). Purchase some to go.

Your next stop has to be at our sparkling organic wine capital: **Summerhill Pyramid Winery** (page 31). Here you have an array of international award–winning sparkling wines and a true pyramid to marvel at. Eat lunch at the fabulous organic **Sunset Bistro**, which has views like crazy.

Pop your last cork of the day at the spectacular **Mission Hill Family Estate Winery** (page 59). Set on a hilltop of West Kelowna, this castle-like estate has a must-visit tasting room and shop. There is a dynamic repertoire of wines to taste, including the new Exhilaration Brut. Book dinner at **Mission Hill's Terrace Restaurant** as the fabulous finale to your sparkling weekend!

Island Pinot Noirist Tour

Pinot Noir is known as the heartbreak grape because of its very fragile personality. Luckily, this finicky grape seems to thrive in BC. Plan two tours to taste BC's wine stars in all of their glory.

The first is the Cowichan Bay area of Vancouver Island, which has some dynamite Pinot Noirs on offer. To get here, you can fly into Victoria and drive roughly an hour to your destination, or take the ferry from Vancouver to Nanaimo or Victoria. It takes about 45 minutes to get to Cowichan Bay from either ferry terminal. Book accommodation at the **Grouse House** at beautiful **Blue Grouse Estate Winery** for a full wine-country immersion.

Day One

After coffee and a bite to eat at the local **True Grain** in Cowichan Bay, enjoy the drive to Duncan for your first tasting of the day (unless you are already staying there!), the award-winning Quill Pinot Noir at **Blue Grouse Estate Winery** (page 217). You will fall in love with this estate.

For lunch, you are in for a treat at **Vigneti Zanatta** (page 213). If you are lucky, you can taste their limited-release Allegria Brut Rosé, which is made with their estate-grown Pinot Noir in the charming farmhouse tasting room. Then take a seat on the porch overlooking the vineyard and enjoy a plate of cheese and charcuterie with your glass of wine.

In the afternoon, wind your way over to **Alderlea Vineyards** (page 209) for a taste of their estate Pinot Noir at their true farmgate winery experience. Plan for a pizza night at **Pizzeria Prima Strada** in Cobble Hill.

Day Two

Start your day with a delicious coffee and danish at **Drumroaster Coffee** in Cobble Hill. Then head over to **Venturi-Schulze Vineyards** (page 221) for a taste of their fine Pinot Noir and a sampling of their astonishing estate-made balsamic vinegar!

Your next stop is **Unsworth Vineyards** in Mill Bay (page 225) for a tasting, followed by lunch at their gorgeous restaurant. Save some time to wander around the beautiful gardens and vineyards.

Book your afternoon tasting and wine tour at **Averill Creek Vineyard** in Duncan. This family-run 40-acre estate winery is all about crafting incredible Pinot Noir. For dinner, head to the charming **Hudson's on First**. They also make up custom picnic baskets!

Okanagan Pinot Noirist Tour

The Kelowna area is home to some of the province's best Pinot Noirs. The terroir here seems to suit the high-maintenance vines. Plan to stay in Kelowna and do a day trip south to visit some amazing Pinot Noirists.

Day One

After breakfast at your hotel, make a beeline to **SpearHead Winery** (page 35). This boutique-style winery is making some beauties. Now with Pinot Noir–focused winemaker Grant Stanley on their team, they are taking their wines to the next level.

On the way down the hill, stop at **Sperling Vineyards** (page 43) for a taste of their bio-dynamic wines and a history lesson on this pioneering family. Make time to wander around their amazing vineyard labyrinth.

Prepare to be dazzled by the views and the wines at the legendary **Quails' Gate Winery** (page 51), owned and operated by one of BC's first wine families. The **Old Vines Restaurant** is a stunning vineyard venue—take in the vineyard and lake views while enjoying their award-winning wines. After lunch, stroll up to their impressive tasting room to sample their Pinot Noir and do a shop.

Day Two

Grab a quick breakfast at the **Waterfront Café** or the **Bohemian Café** in downtown Kelowna, then get started on the 1½-hour drive alongside Okanagan Lake to **Covert Farms Family Estate** in Oliver (page 133). Taste the wines, shop for veggies and feast your eyes on this glorious third-generation farm operation.

Eat lunch at **Liquidity Winery** in Okanagan Falls. They have beautiful wines to taste, including two luscious Pinot Noirs. Next, wander over to **Meyer Family Vineyards** (page 115) and prepare for some Pinot pleasure with a tasting of their range of fine wines. To keep the wine flowing all year, join their wine club.

On the way home, pop into **Roche Wines** (page 91) to taste their incarnation of Pinot Noir. The husband-and-wife winemakers have a strong history of French winemaking. And while in Penticton, stop at the **BC Wine Info Centre** and chat with their knowledgeable staff. They would be happy to build you a mixed case of Pinot Noir stars to take home!

Head back to the hotel to relax and then enjoy dinner at one of Kelowna's restaurant stars, **Waterfront Wines** or **RauDZ Regional Table**— both feature wonderful local wine lists. If you are staying in Penticton, **TIME Winery & Kitchen** (page 83), owned by the McWatters family (Okanagan wine royalty), is the place to eat!

Blue Tooth, a Big Red Tour

Okay, palates, prepare for the big hitters, the ones that turn your teeth blue: the big reds of the Okanagan.

Plant yourself in Okanagan South. There are gorgeous winery accommodations at **Burrowing Owl Estate Winery** and **Hester Creek Estate Winery**, or you could book in the Similkameen at **Forbidden Fruit Winery**'s house rental or at the soon-to-be-finished accommodations at **Corcelettes Estate Winery**. If you are driving from the West Coast, you can travel either the Coquihalla or Crowsnest to get to the Similkameen. The nearest airport is Penticton, or you could take a Helijet!

Pack your whitening toothpaste, but wear those blue teeth as a badge of pride.

Day One

Start your tasting day in Osoyoos at **Moon Curser Vineyards** (page 175). Enjoy their marvellous view of Anarchist Mountain, and their power lineup of showstopper wines, including their award-winning blend, Border Vines.

Trek to Oliver and to **Burrowing Owl Estate Winery** (page 165) for a tasting. Lunch on their gorgeous patio restaurant for an unforgettable wine-country view and experience.

After lunch, head to **Quinta Ferreira Estate Winery** (page 141) for a tasting of their reds. Take a seat on their lovely patio to rest and soak in the vineyard ambiance.

Your next stop is **vinAmité Cellars** (page 149), a small winery with a big heart and fabulous wines. Taste an array of their estate-grown vin rouge, including their delicious Compass blend. They also make their own charcuterie! It's perfect to take away with you or enjoy with a glass on their charming patio.

End your day with dinner on the patio at **Terrafina at Hester Creek by RauDZ**. Before dinner, walk up to the winery for a tasting, including big red beauties Garland and the Judge.

Day Two

Take a drive to the gorgeous Similkameen this morning and start your day at **Corcelettes Estate Winery** (page 187). Please your palate with their buzzed-about reds, like the Menhir blend, and whack a few golf balls off the vineyard tee.

Make a stop at **Forbidden Fruit Winery** (page 179) to taste the organic reds made for their Earth Series and Dead End wines. Of course, you have to taste the fruit wines too! Stock up on wine and organic fruit here.

Enjoy a delicious Indian lunch at **Desert Hills Estate Winery's Black Sage Bistro** (page 161) before you head to the tasting room to experience some of our very best Okanagan reds. The star here is the Mirage blend.

Up the hill a bit is **Fairview Cellars**, where winemaking legend Bill Eggert, who knows all things Cabernet (he's known locally as the Cab Man), grows and makes exceptional reds. He also plays the piano in the tasting room if you hit the right day.

Dine at **Miradoro Restaurant at Tinhorn Creek** and enjoy gourmet wine-country cuisine with amazing views. Or, if you have a group, book a very special private dinner experience with Chef Chris Van Hooydonk at **Backyard Farm**!

Practising Chardonnayism

This gorgeous white varietal has returned to the spotlight after a terrible time of misunderstanding. BC has many versions of Chardonnay to offer—from oaked to unoaked, steely to buttery, and everything in between. Here are suggestions on how best to practice your #Chardonnayism in the Okanagan.

Base yourself in Okanagan South for this Wine Adventure. **Spirit Ridge Resort** has beautiful rooms and **Nk'Mip Cellars** is right next door, so there's no need to wander far for one of your stops. You can drive or fly into Penticton airport for this adventure.

Day One

Enjoy the morning drive to **Bartier Bros.** for the first tasting of the day.

The glamourous **Black Hills Estate Winery** nearby has a beautiful Chard, and lunch can be enjoyed on their view patio. Prepare to be dazzled in Chardonnay heaven at storied **CheckMate Artisanal Winery** (page 157)—the prices are high end, but so are the wines.

Return to your nesting place at Spirit Ridge and walk over to **Nk'Mip Cellars** (page 169) for your final tasting. The Reserve Chardonnay is a treat!

You can purchase a bottle and barbecue dinner on your suite patio, or dine at the beautiful **Nk'Mip patio restaurant.**

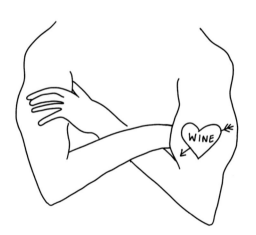

Day Two

In the morning, drive to Okanagan Falls and **Nighthawk Vineyards** (page 125) to enjoy their lovely Chardonnay at their unique log house tasting room.

Your next stop is **Meyer Family Vineyards** (page 115), who are famous for their different levels of Chardonnay. Relax on the beautiful vineyard setting and views of Peach Cliff Mountain.

Head into Penticton, a quick 15 minutes away, for a tasting and lunch downtown at **TIME Winery & Evolve Cellars** (page 83). This beautiful urban winery is owned by the legendary McWatters family. No surprise, the Chardonnay is delicious.

After lunch, a quick hop over to Naramata gets you to **La Frenz Winery** (page 99) to taste their epic Chardonnays (do try everything here—the Sauvignon Blanc and Viognier are fantastic).

Upper Bench Winery & Creamery (page 87) (yes, they make wine AND cheese!) has a fabulous Chardonnay. While you're here, buy cheese to pair with for later.

Now you should have a trunk full of delicious Chardonnay to take home and share!

Riesling Rendezvous: A Very Racy Wine Tour

Poor Riesling's reputation as a syrupy dessert wine stuck for a long time—but now it is receiving a well-deserved return to the spotlight (although it never left it in the Alsace region, Germany and Austria), enjoying a rebirth and a new fan base of foodies, as it makes for fabulous wine pairings. Riesling is crisp, aromatic, fruity, refreshing and even racy and bracing. BC creates a wide range of this beauty, and this tour covers some of the greats.

You can fly into either Penticton or Kelowna—if you stay in Kelowna, do the tour in reverse.

Day One

Start at Summerland's **8th Generation Vineyard** (page 79), where eighth-generation German winemaker Bernd Schales and his wife Stefanie are sharing their legacy of old-world winemaking. Obviously, they know how to make amazing Riesling!

Drive to Okanagan Falls and their beloved **Wild Goose Vineyards** (page 119) for your next Riesling. Another German family, the Krugers, are pioneers in Okanagan winemaking. Stay for lunch here at the **Smoke & Oak Bistro**—don't miss the vine-smoked pork ribs.

Synchromesh Wines is one of the small but mighty wineries on the BC wine list, an operation with a big heart and big awards. The Riesling is a star.

Day Two

You may have to book an appointment to taste the uber award-winning Riesling from **Tantalus Vineyards**. This stunning winery offers lake views and excellent wines.

Carry on down the side of beautiful Okanagan Lake to visit the famed **CedarCreek Estate Winery** (page 21). After your wine tasting, tuck into a glorious lunch in their new restaurant. You may or may not be able to visit **Martin's Lane Winery** (page 25) above this estate. They specialize in creating an exclusive line of top-tier Riesling and Pinot Noir.

After lunch, pop down the street to **St. Hubertus & Oak Bay Estate Winery**. This is one of the sites of the very first vineyards planted in Kelowna, back in 1928! Since 1984, the Gebert family have been creating buzzworthy wines, especially their Riesling. If you are in a group, make sure to prebook the tasting. St. Hubertus also has a helipad and can be visited as part of a very high-end wine tour via www.skyhelicopters.ca or www.valhallahelicopters.com.

Rosé ALL Day

In North America we have finally realized what the French have known all along: rosé is the ultimate summer sipper. These days, everything is coming up rosé in BC, with many delicious choices in every shade of pink.

Base yourself in the Okanagan for this Winey Weekend. Book an Airbnb or stay on a vineyard at the **D'Angelo Estate Winery** (page 107) Guest House, and drive or fly into Penticton airport to begin this adventure. Prepare to pull up a patio chair and drink #RoseAllDay.

Day One

Hit the rosé trail early and kick off with Vaila at **Le Vieux Pin Winery** (page 145) in Oliver. Head back to **JoieFarm Winery** in Naramata to enjoy a tasting, including their famous Re-Think Pink! rosé, then stay for an al fresco lunch. **Le Comptoir at Joie Picnique** serves a delicious meal among the fruit trees in their beautiful heritage orchard.

A couple of minutes up the road you will find **Lock & Worth Winery**. Their tasting room is located at the famous **Poplar Grove Cheese**, where you can enjoy a sip of their Cabernet Franc rosé and purchase cheese to make up a board to take back to the guesthouse for later.

If you are staying at **D'Angelo Estate Winery** Guest House, then this is the ideal place to finish the day. Rosalina Rosé is named for their beloved nonna and is made from their estate Merlot grapes. You can also take a bottle back to your guesthouse and enjoy it there. Book dinner at the **Bistro at Hillside Winery** up the road.

Day Two

Shimmy over to Summerland for the day. You can have a stroll around town and have coffee and a bite to eat at **True Grain**, then start your tasting day with the delicious **TH Wines** Rosé. TH, aka Tyler Harlton, is a local producer whose small-lot wines are getting plenty of buzz.

Next, head to **Silkscarf Winery** (page 75) for a taste of their lineup, including the lovely Saignée rosé, which is crafted from their Shiraz and Pinot Noir grapes. This wine pairs perfectly with a sunny Okanagan day.

Stop by **The Oven at Upper Bench Winery & Creamery** (page 87) for a delicious pizza lunch, and while you're there, be sure to sample some of their rosé.

For dinner, you can pick up a few picnic items along your journey and dine under the stars at your vineyard venue at **D'Angelo**.

HOORAY FOR ROSÉ ALL DAY!

Other Wineries to Visit

This book provides a small snapshot into the huge community of wineries available to visit in BC. Here are a few more spectacular places to investigate and to add to your wine trip adventures!

Okanagan Central

O'Rourke's Peak Cellars
www.orourkespeakcellars.com
The most epic winery project in progress with incredible wine caves.

Arrowleaf Cellars | www.arrowleafcellars.com
A stunning lake view with delicious food offerings.

Frind Estate Winery | www.frindwinery.com
Brand new on the scene, owned by the founder of the Plenty of Fish dating site.

The Hatch | thehatchwines.com
Arguably the most fun and whimsical winery experience in the Okanagan. The wines are good, too!

Tantalus Vineyards | tantalus.ca
One of Kelowna's epic views on a pioneer vineyard known for its benchmark Riesling.

St Hubertus & Oak Bay Estate Winery
www.st-hubertus.bc.ca
Organic and sustainable, and known for their Marechal Foch.

TH Wines | www.thwines.com
A small-batch winemaker with a cult following.

JoieFarm | joiefarm.com
An al fresco dining experience in an old Naramata apple orchard. Famous for their rosé.

Lake Breeze Vineyards | lakebreeze.ca
Offers a gorgeous patio restaurant surrounded by gardens.

Howling Bluff Estate Wines | www.howlingbluff.ca
Super award-winning Pinot Noirists.

Tightrope Winery | www.tightropewinery.ca
Small but mighty, and with a woman winemaker.

Bench 1775 | www.bench1775.com
Insanely stunning Naramata views from the terrace hanging over Lake Okanagan.

Liquidity Wines | www.liquiditywines.com
Part winery, part restaurant and part art gallery, with an epic view of Okanagan Falls.

Sandhill Wines | www.sandhillwines.ca
This well-known BC brand is housed in a cool urban winery in downtown Kelowna. Known for their Small Lots program.

Stag's Hollow Winery | stagshollowwinery.com
An award-winning and innovative winery, with unusual wines like Dolcetto, Tempranillo and Albarino.

Oliver, Osoyoos & Similkameen Valley

Fairview Cellars | www.fairviewcellars.ca
Bill Eggert is a legend in the industry. He is known as the "Cab Man" for his incredible Cabernet Sauvignon.

Harker's Organics & Rustic Roots Fruit Winery & Cidery | www.harkersorganicsrusticroots.com
A farming family with an iconic fruit stand, they also make fruit wine and cider (some from their over 100-year-old apple tree)!

Clos du Soleil | www.closdusoleil.ca
Organic, biodynamic leaders in natural winemaking.

Orofino Winery | www.orofinovineyards.com
Canada's only strawbale-made winery in an extraordinary setting.

Vanessa Vineyard | vanessavineyard.com
Home to super winemaker and Order of Canada recipient Howard Soon.

Fraser Valley, Vancouver Island & Gulf Islands

Backyard Vineyards | www.backyardvineyards.ca
Enjoy the magical views of the lush Fraser Valley.

Krause Berry Farms & Estate Winery
www.krauseberryfarms.com
Wine and berries and pies . . .

Gehringer Brothers Estate Winery
www.gehringerwines.ca
Pioneers in the industry, their wines have tons of awards and are super affordable.

River Stone Estate Winery
www.riverstoneestatewinery.ca
Once Garagistes, they are known for the red blend, Cornerstone.

Rust Wine Co. | www.rustwine.com
A super cool new(ish) property with delicious food and award-winning wines.

Salt Spring Vineyards
www.saltspringvineyards.com
A beautiful winery on Salt Spring Island? 'Nuff said.

Averill Creek Vineyard | www.averillcreek.ca
Winemaker Andy Johnston is creating fabulous Pinot Noir here.

Thompson Valley, Lillooet, Shuswap & Kootenays

Harper's Trail Estate Winery | www.harperstrail.com
Sitting on a property steeped in ranching history, it also has a patio restaurant with great views.

Celista Estate Winery | www.celistawine.com
A stunning garden setting in the beautiful Shuswap with charming owners.

Recline Ridge Vineyards & Winery
www.reclineridgewinery.com
A lovely lakeside winery making excellent cool climate varieties.

Skimmerhorn Winery & Vineyard
www.skimmerhorn.ca
Lovely patio restaurant celebrating Kootenay cuisine.

Baillie-Grohman Estate Winery
www.bailliegrohman.com
Set with a fabulous backdrop of the Skimmerhorn mountain range.

Garagiste Wine Tour

The Okanagan is home to the Garagiste North Small Producers Wine Festival. The festival celebrates artisan winemakers who are making under 2,000 cases of wine each. These small producers are filled with enthusiasm for their craft, and together they make up a community of likeminded people who are following their dreams. The result is a beautiful symphony of spirit and some amazing winemaking.

Many of these small producers do not (yet!) have a tasting room, but some do. They are spread out across the province, so use this list as a guide for ideas to add on to your wine tour when you are in the area. Remember that the Garagiste North Small Producers Wine Festival is a moment in wine time, so some of the Garagistes may be grown up by the time you get to them. Vive les Garagistes!

Okanagan Central

Nagging Doubt Winery, Kelowna
naggingdoubt.com
Rob & Abbey Westbury

Scorched Earth Winery, Kelowna
www.scorchedearthwinery.ca
Peter & Anita Pazdernik

Niche Wine Co., West Kelowna
www.nichewinecompany.com
James & Johanna Schlosser

Off the Grid Organic Winery, West Kelowna
www.offthegridorganicwinery.com
Travis, Sheri, Nigel & Hayley Paynter

Okanagan South

Lightning Rock Winery, Summerland
www.lightningrockwinery.com
Jordan Kubek & Tyler Knight

Giant Head Estate Winery, Summerland
www.giantheadwinery.com
Jinny Lee & John Glavina

Four Shadows Vineyard & Winery, Penticton
www.fourshadowsvineyard.com
Joka & Wilbert Borren

MOCOJO Wines, Naramata | mocojowines.com
Kon and Dianne Oh

Origin Wines, Naramata | www.originwines.ca
Blake and Daiya Anderson

Oliver, Osoyoos & Similkameen Valley

Lariana Cellars, Osoyoos
www.larianacellars.com
Dan & Carol Scott

Fraser Valley, Vancouver Island & Gulf Islands

Emandare Vineyard, Duncan
www.emandarevineyard.com
Mike & Robin Nierychlo

Thompson Valley, Lillooet, Shuswap & Kootenays

Marionette Winery, Salmon Arm
marionettewinery.com
Jamie Smith

Red Bird Estate Winery, Creston | redbirdwine.com
Remi & Shannon Cardinal

Keep an eye out for these future tasting room announcements: Anthony Buchanan Wines; Birch Block Vineyard; Black Market Wine Co.; Rigour & Whimsy; Winemaker's CUT; Wolfe & Wilde.

Thank You

A HEARTFELT THANK YOU TO THE amazing cast members of this book. All of you epitomize the love and passion of our beautiful BC wine industry. You truly inspire me. Thank you for sharing your treasured recipes with us. Know that through this book, the recipe creators and your families will be celebrated again and again at countless tables of wine lovers. Cheers!

Thank you to my loving parents, family and super supportive husband, Mark Pigott.

Hillary Schell, my talented, beautiful niece, it has been so special to work with you on this project. Your illustrations and font added both beauty and whimsy to the spirit of the book. I will cherish it forever.

To my amazing recipe testing crew: Mom, Nanci Macdonald, Cristi Cooke, Beryl Cooke, Brent Beasley, Heidi and Paula Liakakos and Tammy Renard (chief recipe tester), thank you for being meticulous and for following the rules of recipe testing. I know it is hard!

To Tammy Renard, Claire Sear and Mark Pigott, my photo assistants and reflector holders (seriously, it's harder than it looks), thank you for helping me capture these beautiful people and their food. David McIlvride, thank you for your photograph contributions, your guidance and your ongoing support in my cookbook world.

Thank you to Staub and Zwilling for the gorgeous cookware, to Josie and Paul of Byrns Road Blooms for the stunning dahlias on the cover, to Dawn at Landmark flowers for the fat roses and to Wendy Joyner Yates of Old's Cool Designs for her beautiful stamped silver cutlery. Thank you to Tourism Shuswap, Tourism Kootenays and to Blue Grouse winery for providing me a cozy bed at the end of a long day.

And thank you to Robert, Lindsay P. and Lindsay V. at Appetite by Random House. What an incredible and enriching experience it has been working with you all. Your world class professionalism and dedication to perfection are even more remarkable because they are accomplished with such warmth and inclusiveness. I am so thrilled to be a part of the Appetite family.

A special acknowledgement to the McWatters family for allowing me to photograph the cover on their vineyard. Harry's spirit sparkles through this view.

Index